OPRAH WINFREY

OPRAH WINFREY

A Biography

Helen S. Garson

GREENWOOD BIOGRAPHIES

GREENWOOD PRESS
WESTPORT, CONNECTICUT · LONDON

Library of Congress Cataloging-in-Publication Data

Garson, Helen S.
    Oprah Winfrey : a biography / Helen S. Garson.
       p. cm. — (Greenwood biographies, ISSN 1540–4900)
    Includes bibliographical references and index.
    ISBN 0–313–32339–9 (alk. paper)
    1. Winfrey, Oprah. 2. Television personalities—United States—Biography.
3. Actors—United States—Biography. I. Title. II. Series.
PN1992.4.W56G37   2004
791.4502'8'092—dc 22

                                         2004010669

British Library Cataloguing in Publication Data is available.

Library of Congress Catalog Card Number: 2004010669

ISBN: 0–313–32339–9
ISSN: 1540–4900

First published in 2004

Greenwood Press, 88 Post Road West, Westport, CT 06881
An imprint of Greenwood Publishing Group, Inc.
www.greenwood.com

Printed in the United States of America

The paper used in this book complies with the
Permanent Paper Standard issued by the National
Information Standards Organization (Z39.48–1984).

10 9 8 7 6 5 4 3 2 1

For Neil, Always

CONTENTS

Photo essay follows page 78.

SERIES FOREWORD

In response to high school and public library needs, Greenwood developed this distinguished series of full-length biographies specifically for student use. Prepared by field experts and professionals, these engaging biographies are tailored for high school students who need challenging yet accessible biographies. Ideal for secondary school assignments, the length, format and subject areas are designed to meet educators' requirements and students' interests.

Greenwood offers an extensive selection of biographies spanning all curriculum-related subject areas including social studies, the sciences, literature and the arts, history and politics, as well as popular culture, covering public figures and famous personalities from all time periods and backgrounds, both historic and contemporary, who have made an impact on American and/or world culture. Greenwood biographies were chosen based on comprehensive feedback from librarians and educators. Consideration was given to both curriculum relevance and inherent interest. The result is an intriguing mix of the well known and the unexpected, the saints and sinners from long-ago history and contemporary pop culture. Readers will find a wide array of subject choices from fascinating crime figures like Al Capone to inspiring pioneers like Margaret Mead, from the greatest minds of our time like Stephen Hawking to the most amazing success stories of our day like J. K. Rowling.

While the emphasis is on fact, not glorification, the books are meant to be fun to read. Each volume provides in-depth information about the subject's life from birth through childhood, the teen years, and adulthood. A thorough account relates family background and education, traces personal and professional influences, and explores struggles, accomplishments, and contributions. A timeline highlights the most significant life events against a historical perspective. Bibliographies supplement the reference value of each volume.

ACKNOWLEDGMENTS

My thanks to the following people, without whose enthusiastic assistance I could not have undertaken this work: Lisa Cohen, for newspaper research and computer know-how; Sally Gottlieb for magazine research; the ever-helpful librarians of Montgomery County, Maryland, and Palm Beach County, Florida; and above all, my husband, H. Neil Garson, my most patient reader, editor, and listener.

TIMELINE

1954   Oprah Gail Winfrey, the illegitimate child of Vernita Lee and Vernon Winfrey, was born on January 29 in Kosciusko, Mississippi, where she lived until the age of six with grandparents Hattie Mae and Earless Lee.

1960   Oprah went to live with her mother, Vernita, and half sister, Patricia, in Milwaukee, Wisconsin.

1962   Oprah spent a brief time with her father, Vernon, and stepmother, Velma, in Nashville, Tennessee, and attended East Wharton Elementary School in Nashville.

1963   While living with her mother in Milwaukee, Oprah was raped by a cousin and victimized by other sexual predators.

1968   Oprah received a scholarship to attend Nicolet High School in Milwaukee.
        Vernita sent Oprah back to Nashville, where she gave birth to a son who died shortly afterwards. She attended East Nashville High School, from which she graduated in 1971. While there, she was a member of the drama club, the National Forensics League, the honor society, and the student council, and was voted the most popular girl of the senior class. She also served as a representative to a White House Conference.

1969   Some time this year, Oprah began to keep a journal, which she still maintains.

1970   While representing Nashville station WVOL, Oprah won the contest for Miss Fire Prevention. She also was selected as the first Miss Black Tennessee.

1971   Oprah graduated from high school and won a scholarship to
        Tennessee State University. She was hired to read the weekend
        news at radio station WVOL and on occasion read the weekday
        news.

1973   After working for a time at station WLAC, Oprah went to its
        television station, WLAC-TV.
        She left college before graduating to accept a job in Baltimore.

1976   At station WJZ-TV in Baltimore, she worked as a reporter and
        coanchor of an evening news program. There she met produc-
        tion assistant Gayle King who became and remains her closest
        friend.

1978   At WJZ-TV Oprah was taken off the evening program and
        made cohost of the morning show *People Are Talking*.

1984   Oprah accepted a job in Chicago as host of AM *Chicago*.

1985   Oprah met Stedman Graham, who was to become her "signifi-
        cant other." She also met Quincy Jones, who offered her the role
        of Sophia in *The Color Purple*, for which she became an Oscar
        nominee.

1986   Her program was renamed *The Oprah Winfrey Show*. It had been
        purchased by the King Brothers Corporation and was nationally
        syndicated.
        Oprah also appeared in the movie *Native Son*, a film based on
        the Richard Wright novel.
        She purchased her Chicago penthouse condominium on the
        lakefront.
        Oprah was a guest at the marriage of her friend Maria Shriver to
        Arnold Schwarzenegger in Hyannis, Massachusetts.

1987   More than a decade after leaving Tennessee State University,
        Oprah was granted a degree in speech and drama and delivered
        the commencement address.

1988   Named Broadcaster of the Year by the International Television
        and Radio Society, Oprah was the youngest person to receive
        the award.
        She began to produce her show after gaining ownership and
        control of it.
        Naming her production company Harpo, she purchased the stu-
        dio facilities, becoming the first black woman to own a studio
        and production company.
        She bought a farm in Indiana. In later years she purchased two
        other homes, one in Colorado and one in California.

Her friend and assistant, Billy Rizzo, died of AIDS, the disease that was to kill her half brother.

1989   Jeffrey Lee died of AIDS.

        With another investor, Oprah opened a restaurant, The Eccentric.

1990   Oprah produced the television series *The Women of Brewster Place*, which was dropped after 10 weeks. She also produced and appeared in the film *Listen Up: The Lives of Quincy Jones*.

1992   Oprah made the documentary *Scared Silent*.

        She met Bob Greene, who became her fitness trainer and friend.

1993   Oprah appeared in the television film *There Are No Children Here*, which she also produced.

        President Clinton signed the National Child Protection Act that Oprah had initiated.

1995   Knopf published *In the Kitchen with Rosie*, a cookbook written by Oprah's chef with some input from Oprah.

        Bob Greene's book *Make the Connection* was published under the names of Bob Greene and Oprah Winfrey.

        Oprah ran in and finished the 25-mile Marine Corps Marathon.

1996   Oprah was given the George Peabody Individual Achievement Award.

        She produced *Waiting to Exhale*.

        Texas cattlemen brought a suit against Oprah for disparaging beef.

        Oprah met Dr. Phil McGraw in Texas, where he became one of her advisers.

        The book club became part of the television show.

1997   Oprah created the "Angel Network."

        Oprah appeared in and produced the television film *Before Women Had Wings*.

        Oprah gave the commencement address at Wellesley College, from which Stedman Graham's daughter was graduating.

        Art Smith became Oprah's chef and wrote a cookbook.

1998   *Oprah Winfrey Presents* produced the television miniseries *The Wedding* starring Halle Berry.

        Dr. McGraw joined Oprah's television show.

        Oprah received a Lifetime Achievement Daytime Emmy Award.

        Oprah starred in and produced the movie *Beloved*.

        She was described in *Time* as one of the twentieth-century's "most influential people."

1999   CBS Corporation bought the King Production Company.
        Oprah bought a share of the Oxygen Cable Network.
        Oprah's company presented the television film *Tuesdays with Morrie*.

2000   O magazine was launched; the international edition of the magazine was published a few months later.
        Oprah won the beef defamation suit.

2002   Harpo Productions developed a program for Dr. McGraw.
        Oprah was awarded an honorary doctorate from Princeton University.
        Oprah received the Bob Hope Humanitarian Award.
        Oprah and Stedman stayed at the home of Nelson Mandela in South Africa.
        The book club was discontinued.

2003   Oprah received the Marion Anderson Award.
        Oprah joined with a number of world-famous people to celebrate Mandela's eighty-fifth birthday.
        Oprah's half sister, Patricia Lee Lloyd, died of a drug overdose.
        The book club was reborn.
        Oprah became the first black American billionaire.

Chapter 1

THE WORLD AND OPRAH

"Oprah" is a person so well known that a last name seems almost unnecessary. Like other stars also easily identified by first names—Madonna, Ali—she is immediately recognized. Because the word "Oprah" means instant cognizance, we expect people, if only occasionally, to have watched her daily television program, seen her movies, or read the books she recommends or O, her magazine. But even if they've done none of these things, they are able to place her. When news media reported the possibility of former President Clinton becoming a talk show host, amusing comparisons were made that he could be "a future Oprah." And, in 1998, during Clinton's administration, when his Secretary of State, Madeline Albright, failed during an "Oprah-style" meeting to convince an audience in Ohio about the need to rid the world of Saddam Hussein, *The National Review* humorously suggested that the desired results would have been achieved if Oprah herself had advocated the action.

Simple references to "Oprah" or "Oprah Winfrey" do not have to be explained, even if the news is from foreign countries. A *Baltimore Sun* reporter, sending in news from Beijing, China, tells of the widening influence of America. In addition to material things, there are the cultural aspects of this influence; for example, Beijing housewives watch installments of *Oprah*. In Arlington, Virginia, a Vietnamese immigrant's favorite television show is *Oprah*. Audiences in 107 countries around the world see the program, the leading talk show for 18 years, in spite of its numerous rivals. Abroad, the daily program is viewed by several hundred thousand South African women, most of them white, in a country where the white population is only eight percent of the total. Oprah's appeal crosses racial lines everywhere. It seems as if much of the world and all of America recalls something about her, perhaps more than we do of historic figures, current politicians, scholars, artists, or composers.

On *The West Wing*, the award-winning television program about the American presidency, a member of the fictional presidential staff scoffingly rejects the notion that the president must confess things as if he were on *The Oprah Winfrey Show*. The writers of *The West Wing* presume that the audience will understand and perhaps laugh at the allusion to the entertainer's confessional style. That same belief prompted columnists who write disparagingly of various programs or daily events, major or minor, to use the term "Oprah-ization." Telling of the impact of *Court TV* on the American public, reporters note the addictive quality that plays on the "basest instincts" of the audience, calling the essence of the show "pure Oprah." It is an essence that sells. Reviewing the memoir *Call Me Crazy*, by actress Anne Heche, writer Jabari Asim disparages Heche's message about learning to love one's self, saying it could be found any afternoon on the *Oprah* show or by a "growing horde of imitators." Politicians are said to recommend that some of their colleagues follow her style or "out-Oprah," using the technique of the entertainer to persuade people to support various positions. When former New York Mayor Rudy Giuliani was running for the U.S. Senate, his activities were such that a reporter referred to him as "Oprah-ized."

It seems unlikely or almost impossible to pass a day without seeing or hearing some passing reference to Oprah. Frequently that reference is a stretch, playing on Oprah's celebrity. An example of that may be seen in the table of contents of a Sunday magazine section of *The New York Times*. Inside the magazine the actual article was about a psychic talk show that falls under the category sci-fi, and, except for the sometimes outré theme of a particular *Oprah* presentation, bears no resemblance to the *Oprah* program, which is touted to focus on real life; nonetheless her name appears in the table of contents' description of the article. The prominent placement of Oprah's name is something of a ploy, but it is good business, for it captures many a viewer's eye and interest, suggesting that there is sustenance for the Oprah follower. In one issue, above the masthead of *The Palm Beach Post*, two items, with pictures, call attention to "Accent," the entertainment, leisure, and style segment of the paper. One photo is of Oprah, along with a tantalizing statement about life's "simple truths," words intended to arouse the reader's interest in a particular column. Yes, Oprah is interested in "simple truths," but nothing more is said about her. Would we skip the column if Oprah's face didn't capture our attention?

Very likely. But here, too, is another gambit, a type of advertisement for an inspirational book. The Oprah connection, made by a religion writer, is through mention of her name, along with those of two other well-known figures, as people who found the book "life changing."

Not only do entertainment columns frequently talk of Oprah and her activities, but so do articles about Congress and the White House. During President Bill Clinton's administration an informal title, the "Oprah Bill," was given to a child protection bill he signed into law. The designation made a well-deserved connection, for the law came about after long and intense efforts, including Oprah's financial involvement in hiring attorneys, to protect children from sexual predators.

News reports about wealthy Americans frequently single her out because of her popularity and fame and compare her career to that of others. Articles may refer to Oprah's financial astuteness, although she jokingly speaks of her inability to read a balance sheet. When the "cosmetic empress" Mary Kay (Ash) died in November 2001, the obituary in the *Washington Post* noted Mary Kay's importance in revealing to women such as Oprah an understanding of the methods that could bring about great business success; for Kay and later for Oprah, one of these methods was the involvement of groups in their activities.

Over the years, light-hearted sightings of the entertainer and serious news reports have taken note of Oprah's presence. A typical example of fluff dispatches occurred when a columnist, writing in 1992 about fads in American culture, mentioned a television segment that displayed Oprah taking lambada lessons. However, other aspects of the multifaceted star are also part of the Oprah phenomenon. The sober, grave, yet spontaneously warm traits of the superstar led a *Newsweek* columnist to designate her as "daytime's queen of empathy." That spirit of caring often comes through in diverse ways. When the terrorist attacks of September 11, 2001, were the only subject of the media, Oprah, along with other celebrities, was prominently featured as a participant in the healing process, using her daily program as a vehicle toward that end. Oprah also appeared in an event with First Lady Laura Bush, who, in the aftermath of those strikes against America, became a more visible figure than ever before. Recounting the week's activities of the quiet and somewhat nonpolitical Mrs. Bush, a reporter specifically listed the name Oprah Winfrey as the person who held hands with Mrs. Bush in their shared grief over the thousands of lives lost in the assault. For weeks after the horrific events Oprah appeared to be everywhere, taking on more than ever the national role of therapist to a troubled country.

MS magazine once repeated a fan's accolade, labeling Oprah the American psychiatrist who is "most accessible and honest." Nevertheless, not all descriptions are as flattering. Articles in diverse arts and leisure sections of newspapers or magazines have referred to her with some ambiguity as "Queen Oprah," "media empress," "Empress Oprah," and even "Saint Oprah." Critic David Zuarink classified her as "a czarina of popular culture." Her fluctuating weight never fails to make the news, particularly the tabloid news. Cruel comparisons and descriptions abound, and although entertainers seem to be fair game, some of the remarks about Oprah are in poor taste; exaggerating her size—labeling her as an overweight "black Cinderella"; or bearing a resemblance to the hefty late singer, Sophie Tucker, or the large movie star, Hattie McDaniel who played the simpering maid to Vivian Leigh's Miss Scarlet in *Gone with the Wind*.

In a review of *Winchell: Gossip, Power, and the Culture of Celebrity*, Neil Gabler's 1994 book about the late gossip columnist Walter Winchell, Gary Wills theorizes that the "Winchellizing" of America more than 70 years ago prepared us for the "Oprah-izing" of our time. Daphne Merkin, in a review in *The New York Times Book Review* of Alice Miller's mental health book, *The Truth Will Set You Free*, ironically classifies Miller as "the missing link between Freud and Oprah." Inasmuch as the subtitle of Miller's book is *Overcoming Emotional Blindness and Finding Your True Adult Self*, one may readily understand Merkin's use of the Oprah connection, for Merkin speaks of the movement from "the cloistered offices of therapists" to a larger "user-friendly" environment. Whether the environment of the *Oprah* show is always user-friendly is debatable, but it is a larger and far less expensive venue than a psychiatric office.

In contrast to the assessment of some writers, public praise is often hyperbolic. On the other hand, the evaluations of critics tend to be muted, except from columnists whose work is exclusively concerned with television. With only a few exceptions, the tone behind the brief or general articles is friendly. However, even when it is unfriendly, or tongue in cheek, the implication is clear: Oprah's national and international celebrity has made her someone to be reckoned with. And, as such, she is fair game.

Oprah's fame is such that we might expect to find library shelves filled with all kinds of biographies about her, but this assumption turns out to be incorrect. Although there are biographies, they are not "all kinds." A few out-of-print adult books of earlier vintage—published in the mid-eighties to mid-nineties—and some very short juvenile works exist. Writing styles differ, but the works fall into two main categories; one is biography, the other "sayings." A problem with several of the publications, particularly those that collect "sayings," is the lack of certain dates. This lack is a significant problem. Some statements without dates might lead one to believe something to be true of the mature Oprah whereas she, like most of us, might well have altered her views about some matters over a period of years and sometimes with frequency.

Unfortunately, careless but not insignificant errors also appear. An entry in an encyclopedia erroneously lists the paternal rather than the maternal grandmother as the person with whom Oprah spent her early years; a 1990s biography lists the wrong birth date of the entertainer. Another claims that Oprah's mother married a man with whom she had a longtime relationship, whereas, in fact, she never married. One describes her as "short," a description completely at odds with reality; Oprah is five foot six. Tabloids may present a special problem because their sources of information are typically "friends" who are never identified.

Even before opening some of the books about Oprah, the reader is confronted with titles that usually contain words similar to those found in advertisements: "wonderful" and "remarkable," as well as "love" and "real." Such preconditioning has the hype and exaggerated sounds of a television presentation, even though these books are not authorized; so far, no book is authorized. Unlike most monthlies, Oprah's own magazine, O, rarely prints any faultfinding "Letters to the Editor," which suggests that readers who take the time to write in have nothing critical to say about the articles. Although few people would question America's affection for the entertainer or her impressive role socially and culturally, touting her constantly in books and articles in such hyperbolic language contributes to an adverse effect that actually is diminishing, at least as far as critics are concerned.

Bits and pieces about Oprah abound in magazines and newspapers. Additionally, there are books about her diet or exercise programs and lists of clubs or Web sites that specialize in Oprah's book choices or interests. The publication of her magazine, O, monthly in America and bimonthly internationally, is comparatively recent. It is a vehicle belonging partly to and controlled by Oprah as much as her television program. Like the rare interviews she has granted to the media, other information about Oprah that reach the reading or listening audience are facts that Oprah has chosen—either by sharing them herself or by authorizing others to share them.

If we are to believe the statements issued by Oprah's public relations people, she plans to retire from her daily television program within the next few years. However, she has made that same declaration several times; the date keeps changing and so does Oprah's mind. The audience will know only when it actually occurs. But television for Oprah is more than a vehicle for her daily show; she is an actress as well as a producer of television movies. Further, Hollywood films continue to interest her, although, as with plans to retire, she changes her mind about her role in that industry. And, the growing popularity of her magazine O undoubtedly will influence her later professional decisions. Whatever her future options, the likelihood is that they will involve the entertainment world in one form or another, perhaps acting, directing, or producing. Oprah's great wealth will allow her to make choices. As for her personal life, it probably will continue to interest tabloid writers and readers. For the tabloids she is almost an industry, and should she ever retire completely, they will lose a valuable commodity.

Chapter 2

LIFE IS A JOURNEY

Mississippi, historically one of the poorest states in the nation, has made more racially based political news than its sister southern states. In spite of its role as an important focal point of the civil rights movement in the twentieth century, it did not move as quickly or as well into acceptance of black and white integration. In Mississippi, there remains a strong resistance to numerous changes that have occurred in race relations and laws. In the second year of the new century, a political battle ensued over remarks by Trent Lott, then Republican majority leader in the U.S. Senate. The senator, in a speech praising the retiring centenarian senior senator, Strom Thurmond of South Carolina, appeared nostalgic for a pre-integration world of separate restaurants, toilets, and seating on trains and buses. The angry national uproar following his speech did not extend to the area of Mississippi that had given birth to and elected Senator Lott. In fact, during the Senate's Christmas recess, he was welcomed home as a hero, an episode widely reported on by the media. However, when the Senate subsequently found his views an embarrassment, Senator Lott resigned as a leader.

Mississippi is also the birthplace of television star Oprah Winfrey, a black entertainer of world fame, one of the richest women not only in America but on the planet, and a woman awarded honors of every kind for her own work and also for her philanthropic, educational, and social efforts. Mississippi also was the early home of another idol of the entertainment world, Elvis Presley, who made musical history, and who, after his death, assumed mythic proportions.

Although never known for its cultural life, Mississippi is also the birthplace of three of America's great literary figures, William Faulkner, Eudora

Welty, and Richard Wright; both Faulkner and Welty lived most of their lives in the state. Wright, though, went north, following the path of numerous black people who sought what they hoped would be friendlier, more hospitable surroundings. For most of the twentieth century, other southern states—Georgia, Louisiana, Tennessee, Alabama, and Virginia—provided more fertile ground for writers: novelists and essayists Robert Penn Warren, Truman Capote, and Walker Percy; poet, literary critic, novelist Allan Tate; short-story writers Katherine Ann Porter and Flannery O'Connor; poet Langston Hughes; poet, memoirist, and Oprah's dear friend, Maya Angelou; Zora Neale Hurston, whose novel *Their Eyes Were Watching God* is beloved by Oprah; and, Harper Lee, childhood friend of Capote's and author of another book Oprah has named a favorite, *To Kill a Mockingbird*. Oprah often speaks of the books that affected her most in growing up. Many came from the literary list of outstanding southern writers, traditional as well as more contemporary poets, literary critics, novelists, playwrights, and essayists.

Of particular interest in the cultural study of these writers is the great biographical divide between the races and the many similarities within each racial group. Black writers inform us of their suffering and oppression caused by white people, in addition to portraying the wretchedness and despair of family life. Certainly, white southern writers also explore the tragedies of black people and their families as well as their own individual dysfunctional family relationships but different from the writing of white southern writers is an additional common, sometimes biographical, thread running through the work of many black authors: illegitimacy, desertion, abandonment, promiscuity, and sexual abuse. When in adulthood Oprah and some of her friends have spoken of these matters, their words reflect the books, poems, and stories that are part of America's literary and cultural heritage.

The South is famous as the birthplace of multiple kinds of music, the most familiar being jazz and country. When people speak of New Orleans, the most renowned southern area of the musical past, they evoke reminders of the many musicians, the piano players, the saxophonists, the clarinetists, and the drummers who created jazz, yet, because the majority of the musicians were black and lived during the years of segregation in the South, most of their names have been lost to history. However, according to musicologists, black musical history goes back even further, to the days of slavery, when a unique kind of music evolved.

The South is not only the granddaddy of jazz and country music but also of gospel singing, and it was the sounds of gospel, even though much altered, that provided some of the early background behind mountain music and jazz. Country ballads, familiar to most Americans, are obviously derived from gospel singing. Although both gospel and country music had been sung and played throughout the entire South, these forms of music tend to be associated exclusively with Nashville, Tennessee, the city to which later numerous aspiring artists gravitated. Worldwide, any mention of Nashville conjures up images of certain singers, special types of music, song, and instruments that are the inheritors of mountain culture and gospel music, although those are not the exclusive property of Nashville.

Perhaps the most frequently sung sound in the small towns of the South, gospel music has few famous names tied to it, whereas jazz and country composers and singers are much better known. Nevertheless, gospel music is as much a part of southern culture as ham and grits, biscuits and gravy, fried chicken, and catfish. Children brought up in the small towns of the Bible Belt seemed almost to inhale gospel music along with the weekly churchgoing and rituals. The influence is embedded in their lives, even when they leave the region. Oprah—as well as Elvis, who was also a Mississippian—is a prime example of that effect. Because of her early conditioning, her preferences in music, years after her moves elsewhere, reflect what she regards as the healing influence of gospel sounds, the combination of religion and music. For her, gospel songs are related to faith and hope and healing, and when unhappy, perhaps terrible, things happen, she tells us she turns to gospel music. One such time came after the tragedies of September 11, 2001.

When we turn away from the instant recognition of famous figures from the musical or literary world—after all, their faces often appear on stamps—most of us probably would find it difficult to come up with more than a few names of entertainers associated with the South; it is not usually the area we link with entertainers, other than country, blues, and jazz musicians, in spite of the fact that a great many composers, musicians, singers, and dancers were born there. Yet, cultural history notes they had to head north or west where they gained fame and sometimes—but not always—fortune.

For most Americans, entertainment is associated with the glitter of New York, Hollywood, or Las Vegas. Surely, not Mississippi. However, Oprah Winfrey comes from a little Mississippi town with the unlikely and unfamiliar name of Kosciusko, a city named after the Polish general Tadeusz Kosciuszko/Thaddeus Kosciusko. Known as the "Hero of Two Worlds," he fought for the independence of the colonies in the American

Revolution as well as the independence of his home country, Poland. Much admired for his abilities, he also served with the Continental Congress, which appointed him an engineer with the rank of colonel. Outside of history books and biographies, like many other valorous figures, the general has been forgotten except for the naming of the town that honored his role in eighteenth-century America. Few people remember his historic actions or the fact that he left a legacy to help liberate the slaves.

Kosciusko is only 70 miles north of the capital city, Jackson, but there is almost no resemblance between the two. Little distinguishes Kosciusko from other small farming areas of the state, yet during the early years of the republic, it was an important segment of the frontier route on the road to Nashville. Although people used the Mississippi River whenever possible to transport goods, that method often became too difficult for primitive navigation. The alternative was a land route from Natchez to Nashville, which became known as the "Natchez Trace." Kosciusko still celebrates that period of its history with a Natchez Trace festival every April, even though, unlike other cities along the route, it failed to develop in any significant way. Those other cities became famous as well as heavily populated, but that was not the case for Kosciusko.

The town is located in a region of rivers and frequent rain, with hot and humid weather, pines and flowering trees. In the middle of the twentieth century, when Oprah was born, there was scarcely more variety of work than there had been a hundred or two hundred years earlier. Small farms provided the major source of income. More than half of Mississippi still remains rural, with a 36-percent African American population, larger than that of any other state. At the time of Oprah's birth in 1954, what little industry had existed was almost gone; jobs were scarce and young people, particularly young blacks, who continued to be victims of prejudice and poverty, left if they could, in search of a livelihood. During the time of Oprah's slave ancestors, and during her grandparents' lives, her mother's life, and her own early years, Mississippi was and remains close to the bottom of the economic ladder, in spite of its association with some of the great names in American culture.

The image of the small-town South and its inhabitants flashes through our heads when we think of Mississippians depicted by Faulkner or Welty; but the South is also the worldly Louisiana French Quarter in New Orleans with its ornate balconies and exotic foods and tiny steamy bars, the city where Louis Armstrong sang and played his trumpet; the city in which Truman Capote was born; the Delta river boats on which Armstrong entertained and where the child Truman Steckfus (Capote), going between Louisiana and Alabama, dreamed of becoming a tap dancer; a region of small towns and small wooden churches in which future gospel singers got their start. The South is a unique area that seems to be part of the very blood of most southerners, not only writers and musicians, often in the grounding to much of their work, their thinking, their attitudes, their accents.

Yet unless we listen carefully not only to accents but also to attitudes and read carefully Oprah's words, we tend to make only a few of these associations when we think of her. She lived in two southern states, Mississippi and, except for a few damaging years spent in Milwaukee, Tennessee, for much of her childhood, her teens, and her early twenties. Psychologists and psychiatrists have stated that the first five years determine much of who and what we are, and if we accept that thesis, we must apply the measurement to Oprah, even though in most ways she does not appear to fit the southern image. However, she did attend high school and college in Tennessee, and, after leaving Tennessee, lived and worked in another southern city, Baltimore. But, she claims, she felt little association with her early surroundings, although with the passage of time she has become reconciled to the past, speaking more and more frequently of her Mississippi grandmother. However, she never thought of any southern town or city longingly as home. Unlike many southerners, once she left the South of her youth, she returned only occasionally and never lived there again.

Unhappy childhood memories have led many southern artists to other places, yet they either maintained homes in the South or returned frequently to keep the connection. Mississippian writer Welty settled in her childhood home after a short foray in the life of New York. Even novelist Truman Capote, who declared himself a New Yorker because he'd spent only part of his early years in Alabama, frequently felt the pull of return to Monroeville and New Orleans. Most of his work is southern to the core, created in large measure by a childhood that Oprah's close friend Maya Angelou and others have described as appalling and tragic. Nevertheless, he always felt the need to revisit the southern world. And Maya Angelou herself, who is always identified as a southerner, lived in many parts of this country and elsewhere but finally settled in North Carolina. Yet her friend, Oprah, who spent more years in the South than either Capote or Angelou, turned her back on it, saying at various times throughout the years that she knew when she moved to Chicago at the age of 30 she had found her home.

Needless to say, we must accept her statement; but regardless of that profession, when we look carefully at the person she is, we can't help but recognize the southern roots that are part and parcel of her character and personality: the influence of and love of gospel music; the strong spiritual side of her nature; her deepest affection for southern novels; even her love of southern food and cooking.

Although Oprah always credits two members of her family—her maternal grandmother, Hattie Mae Lee, and her father, Vernon Winfrey—with the qualities that have led to her success, her memories of childhood and early years are filled with more pain and sadness than joy. At times, she claims to have overcome the effects of the past, yet she speaks so frequently of a particular time in her childhood that it seems a wound that has not healed. Those hardships, reflected in many of her interests and activities, are recognizable to all Oprah watchers who also know such things well.

A series of accidents are part of Oprah's heritage; she was born illegitimate, the child of two very young people. Her mother, Vernita Lee, 18 and promiscuous, claimed that a young man named Vernon Winfrey, on leave for two weeks from the Army, had made her pregnant. At times she changed her mind, saying she was uncertain who was responsible. In an interview in a tabloid newspaper, Vernon Winfrey "confessed" he could not have fathered Oprah because he was on Army duty at the time. Service people do go on leave, however, and it's been reported again and again that Winfrey was on leave during that period. Vernita recently modified her story once again, insisting that Vernon is the only person who could be Oprah's father. Winfrey was a 20-year-old father, a soldier stationed at Camp Rucker in Alabama. Apparently with typical carelessness, Vernita Lee didn't notify him about the pregnancy until the child was born. Then, she sent a newspaper announcement along with a request that he mail clothes for the newborn baby.

Like the pregnancy, the name that has become a household word, Oprah, was also an accident. Nobody seemed to know how to spell Orpah, the biblical name the family had chosen from "The Book of Ruth." Although it was written on the official birth certificate, nobody could pronounce it either. People added a "p" before the "r" to the name. In spite of the fact that the official document reads "Orpah," that name isn't used anywhere else, so the spelling became the one we know today.

Some time after her baby's birth at home on the farm, Vernita left the infant with her own mother, Hattie Mae. Oprah's grandfather, Earless Lee, had little to do with the child. Much is made of the fact that Oprah spent her early years with her grandmother, yet she is only one of a number of famous people, some black, others white, who had that experience:

among them, former President Clinton, Tipper Gore, and Justice Clarence Thomas. Oprah remained on the little farm that Grandmother Lee owned in the Mississippi Delta region until the age of six, when she went to live with her mother in Milwaukee, Wisconsin. Different stories are told about the reasons for Oprah's move. One story is that Vernita sent for her, another is that her grandmother found her too difficult to look after, and yet another is that Hattie Mae had become ill. Whatever brought about the child's departure from Mississippi, friends and relatives have talked of the love Hattie Mae had for her first grandchild, who was regarded as unique because of her precocity.

Life on the farm was basic. The grandmother boiled clothes on the screened-in back porch, using a large iron pot since the family had no washing machine. Water had to be drawn from a well. The tiny farmhouse lacked indoor plumbing, so an outhouse was the substitute for an indoor toilet, and one of Oprah's daily chores was emptying the slop jars each morning. In remembering details from her childhood, Oprah has half humorously and half seriously referred to the use of the Sears catalog in the outhouse. From early on she also had to help with the cow, the pigs, and chickens. Because she had no room or bed of her own, she slept with her grandmother in a feather bed, often lying awake terrified that her grandfather would come in during the night and commit a murderous act against both her and her grandmother. An actual incident occurred one night when she was about four years old. An uncontrollable Earless Lee came into the bedroom, and Oprah's grandmother had to rush out into the darkness to scream for help from a neighbor. Though the neighbor was old and blind, Oprah remembers him as a rescuer. In the daytime Grandfather Lee also was a fearsome presence, threatening the child with his cane or throwing various things at her.

Much like life on the farm, her grandmother was rigid and harsh, meting out punishment for any infringement of rules, even for happenings over which the little girl had little or no control. Whippings were part of Oprah's upbringing, in accordance with the old credo "spare the rod and spoil the child." Strongly religious, Hattie Mae Lee spent most of her free time at the Faith-United Mississippi Baptist Church, located close to the farm, where she also took Oprah from her earliest days. Because her grandmother's other preoccupation after religion was reading, even in babyhood Oprah was taught how to read and to memorize passages of the Bible, activities that gained renown for her when she was only a toddler. With the strong discipline at home, only in the local Baptist church was she given the opportunities to express herself. As a result of her ability to recite pieces from the Bible as a very young child, she was called on to do Easter selections. Oprah still remembers some of the recitations, one of which was "Jesus rose on Easter Day, Hallelujah, Hallelujah, all the angels did proclaim." While fanning themselves against the heat of the season and listening to the toddler's recitations, the ladies of the church would praise the little girl to her grandmother, calling her a gifted child. She has said that her first Easter speech was probably made at the Kosciusko Baptist church when she was about three and a half. Only a few years later she was able to recite the entire series of the seven sermons of James Weldon Johnson from "Creation" to "Judgment."

In recalling her early years, Oprah has reflected that at various times she spoke at all the churches in the city of Nashville. When interviewed by evening talk show host, Larry King, she told him she'd been a keynote speaker in many different kinds of places from age 13 on. Although once she became famous, admirers often pointed to her many years of experience in broadcasting as a part of preparation for film work, her entire life actually prepared her for that. So many elements came together ultimately in her career. Her religious fervor in childhood, however, was a mixed blessing, because the hostility of other youngsters to her talents earned her the nicknames "The Preacher" and "Miss Jesus." During the period that she lived with her mother, Vernita, she became known in Milwaukee as "Little Speaker" because of her pious zeal. Not only did she recite sermons and biblical passages, but by age seven, she was declaiming, with full gestures, inspirational poems such as Henley's "Invictus," without understanding a word in any of them.

On the farm, Oprah was lonely, isolated, and friendless. One of her cousins, Alice Cooper, from the same small town, has told of the solitude children felt in those days because the farms were so far from each other that relatives found it difficult to visit back and forth. Oprah envied children who had easier lives, particularly white children, whose families owned television sets and washing machines; children who had store-bought clothing and who could go to movies; children who were not punished for every little misdeed—knowing or unknowing. Even though the whippings she endured were common in her narrow world and time, she has observed that white children rarely were beaten; however, she has humorously remarked, if white girls had to be punished, they got "spanked," whereas black children got "whupped." Without indoor plumbing, not only was her grandmother's so-called washing machine the scrub pot for clothing, but it also served for bathing, which took place only once a week, on Saturdays, in preparation for the Sabbath. Every garment they wore was made at home, and shoes were worn exclusively for Sunday churchgoing. The rest of the time the child went barefoot. Food consisted of what they grew or raised on the farm, with Grandmother Hattie Mae selling eggs to have some cash, as did many a poor southern farm woman for decades, if not centuries. Yet, in spite of the fact that some biographies have called Oprah's life one of extreme poverty, or even so-called grinding poverty, because the grandmother owned a farm, she was able to feed and clothe her family, and they never went hungry.

Visitors to Grandmother Lee's house were adults who expected children to be not only well behaved but silent as well. As a result, Oprah's sole companions were the pigs she helped take care of. Away from the little house, she could read, talk to, and tell stories to them because her restrictive grandmother and her friends believed that Oprah talked too much. Although they all praised the child's articulateness and cleverness in church activities, they did not extend that kind of openness to other places. It is no wonder that by the time she was six she looked forward to living with her mother in Milwaukee.

Her expectations of a different kind of existence were fulfilled but not in the ways she anticipated. Only in adulthood did she recognize how fortunate she had been to live with her grandmother for the first six years of her life; only then could she sort out the love that existed beneath her fear. It took maturity for Oprah to understand that her grandmother had shaped her character, that it was Grandmother Lee who taught her to be strong, to be spiritual—a believer in God. That spiritual quality has never left her, and, during agonizing national times such as the days after September 11, 2001, she shared that spirituality by offering public prayers on her television programs. She developed not only the devotional part of her character from her grandmother but also her ability to reason and her sense of self that was shaken but never lost; the knowledge that she had a place in the world; and, with her later success, a feeling of obligation to help others.

Oprah has said she'll look like her grandmother when she is old, just as she expects to be spiritual in the ways her grandmother was, to be someone who fits into the amen corner. Oprah's mother, Vernita, seems to have lacked all the qualities of her own mother that Oprah admires and cherishes. In fact, Oprah's stepmother, Zelma, who died in 1996, had the strict rules and discipline that made her resemble Grandmother Lee more than Vernita did.

Oprah has never understood why Vernita sent for her. She had no room in her apartment for another person, so that the six-year-old girl had to sleep in the foyer. Vernita was a poor woman who lived on a combination of welfare money and earnings as a maid who cleaned houses; in retrospect she doesn't appear to be someone who could or would take on the burden of raising another child. While Oprah lived on the Mississippi farm, a second illegitimate daughter had been born to Vernita, who also had a third illegitimate child when Oprah was about nine years old. In that household Oprah felt unloved and unwanted, a burden and an outcast, inferior to a half sister she thought prettier because her skin was lighter. In Vernita's home the younger girl was always praised for her looks, whereas Oprah, the more clever one, was never complimented for her intelligence. The owner of the house in which they lived, a Mrs. Miller, preferred the younger child to Oprah, who was convinced it was because the younger girl was light skinned.

From early on, like many other African Americans, Oprah has been conscious of color, not only of race, but of what differences in color could mean in people's lives. When she was a small girl, she envied white children for what she thought of as their easier and more pampered existence, and also because it seemed to her that white children were more beautiful than she was; she envied not just skin color but also noses, lips, and hair. Oprah's longings, of course, were neither unique nor limited to blacks. The Mexican American writer and television critic, Richard Rodriguez, has written of "wanting to be white: that is, to the extent of wanting to be colorless," of wanting to have the feeling of "complete freedom of movement." Being white in America for Rodriguez, for Oprah, and for other minorities of color, meant being free of color. In time, Rodriguez writes, he achieved self-assurance.

As Oprah grew up, her color awareness was not limited to observations about whites. She became conscious, particularly in the all-black college she attended, of subtle and unsubtle patterns among those who had varying shades of blackness. She has said she picked one black college over another, even though she didn't want to be at a school with a student population composed entirely of black students. Never one to accept the idea of black power—particularly the uncompromising form practiced in the seventies when militancy was common—she felt out of place in an atmosphere that was frequently hostile. But aside from the political aspects, the color issue troubled her deeply. Favoritism of many kinds had always been shown to the lighter-skinned person of color, a fact we have learned from the cultural history of race in the United States. During the time of slavery, light-skinned men and women were more likely to become house servants with easier lives than those who were put to work as field hands because their skin was darker. As a dark-skinned African American who had some experience of prejudice once she left Mississippi, Oprah has been outspoken on many occasions in her views of racial snobbery that exists even among blacks.

When she got into college, Oprah felt cynical, if not bitter, about the kinds of color discrimination practiced not only on the outside but also within the black community itself. It was a type of racism she claims she never experienced as a little girl in Kosciusko, which somehow avoided the problems of most southern communities, at least until the sixties when segregationists fought against the new laws that had been passed. However, during Oprah's girlhood in Milwaukee and Nashville she learned of color issues she'd not confronted before. Long after her college years were behind her, she continued to speak of blacks as being "fudge brownies," the color she identifies with herself; "gingerbreads," those black people who have the eye coloring and features of whites; and the group many regard as the most desirable in color, the "vanilla creams," or black people who can "pass" as whites.

Oprah's undeniable interest in black history in the last two decades has taken many forms, in books, movies, and artifacts. Her preferred books often focus on racial issues: slavery, segregation, both overt and covert, violence against blacks (rape, lynching, and other forms of murder), injustice, and the legal system, discrimination in all its varieties. Many of the novels she chose to read over the years are either by black writers, often women—Zora Neale Hurston, Alice Walker, and Toni Morrison, for example—or about black characters, and some of the books have been made into films. Oprah's reading and acting interest meshed when she was asked in 1985 take a role in a movie about African Americans, *The Color Purple*, that became a controversial but financial and popular success. The picture brought her renown, but she had no role in the production. That would change within a few years with Oprah's fame and wealth and the opportunities they brought, producing and acting in films of her choice.

One novel which had haunted her for a long time after reading it, Toni Morrison's *Beloved*, is a work she felt she had to turn into a film because of its historic corrections about ancestry and its humanizing of slavery: living, flesh and blood people whose days were uncertain and agonizing. Oprah played a major role in the movie, having prepared fully to capture the feelings of an eighteenth-century slave. Dressing as a field hand in a replica of the clothing and wearing a blindfold, she walked down a country lane to a plantation house. At another time, in order to grasp the sensations of runaway slaves, she walked through wooded areas as they did in

attempts to escape. The film, which took 10 years to make, was released in
1998. However, regardless of Oprah's dedication to the story, her own acting, money, and publicity, and the famed director Jonathan Demme, it
was a significant failure at the box office, rejected by black audiences and
critics who found it too long and complex. Even with the outpouring of
praise for Oprah's performance as being of "Oscar caliber," and Disney's
enormous efforts to market the picture, nothing could save it. The financial return of approximately $22.5 million was about a third of the cost of
production, but more than the monetary loss then and now disheartens
Oprah, who had a tremendous emotional commitment to the work. So
strong are her ties to *Beloved* that at the top of a marble staircase in her
studios hangs a huge painting of herself from the film.

Because of the interest that had been stirred by *The Color Purple*,
Oprah had high expectations for her later films, several of which preceded
Beloved. A year after her triumph in *The Color Purple*, she followed it with
another African American movie, *Native Son*. However, that picture,
made from the acclaimed autobiography of Richard Wright, turned out to
be a loser both with critics and audience. Rita Kempley of the *Washington
Post* reflects the critiques of others, calling the film "morally medicinal,"
talky, and "preachy," a work that is weighted down by "a sense of its own
nobility." In spite of the flop, the acting bug never left Oprah, and she has
continued to perform and also to finance movies for television and the-
aters. She has experienced both success and failure. The next work she
produced and starred in was a 1989–90 series on television, *The Women of
Brewster Place*, but the series was dropped when a poll showed audience
disinterest, perhaps influenced this time by the denunciation of some
heavy hitters. Although few of the female viewers considered the work
judgmental, the NAACP (National Association for the Advancement of
Colored People) called the portrayal of black men antagonistic. Whereas
white writers were critical of the garrulousness of the characters, some
African American columnists found the programs offensive, reflecting
views reminiscent of those that had been voiced with the showing of
Oprah's first movie. Dorothy Gilliam, a staff writer for the *Washington
Post*, damned the series as "one of the most stereotype-ridden polemics
against black men" and she angrily finds the hackneyed portraits of the
women comparable to the thinking of extreme racists.

Nevertheless, when the movie *Waiting to Exhale* was released in January
1996, Gilliam liked it so much she saw it twice. However, Gregory Kane,
writing for Baltimore's *Sun Sentinel*, found it as offensive as Gilliam had
the Brewster Place series. He angrily depicts Oprah as the "I used cocaine

but the man made me do it" host on her program featuring a group of female stars from the movie, and in bristling language speaks of her and her
guests as "cackl[ing] about how black men do black women wrong in relationships." Nothing was controversial in *Listen Up: The Lives of Quincy
Jones*, a movie about Oprah's dear friend, another film she produced and
starred in the following year. Nevertheless, although the movie *Before
Women Had Wings*, which Oprah's Harpo Productions made for the ABC
network in 1997, was one of her more successful film ventures, some
movie critics found it to be too much of a tearjerker. A year later, under
the listing "Oprah Winfrey Presents," she produced a four-hour miniseries
called *The Wedding*, starring Halle Berry, who would win an Oscar at the
2002 Academy Awards. Then, as if to redeem her judgment, Oprah's most
popular television movie, also under the label "Oprah Winfrey Presents,"
was made in 1999 from Mitch Albom's phenomenally successful book
Tuesdays with Morrie. The film drew 22.5 million viewers, unmatched in
numbers by any other television show for the entire week. The leading
television critic for the *Washington Post*, Tom Shales, who doesn't offer
praise lightly, describes Oprah as someone who "doesn't mess around.... is
no slouch at presenting" or "at anything [else]" she undertakes. Humorously he jokes that she is "not even a slouch at slouching."

Oprah's absorption in the historic life of slaves has led her, like a number of other famous and well-to-do African Americans, such as writer/pro-
fessor Louis Gates, to collecting artifacts of their past. Her purchases of
bills of sale from the days of slave auctions made the news about the time
that Oprah's production failure of *Beloved* was reported.

Clearly, Oprah has not been the first person to discuss the favored
treatment of light- and lighter-skinned Americans. History and literature
have recorded the situation. Essays, plays, novels, and poetry have docu-
mented the stories of lives shattered by the issues of race. William
Faulkner's *Absalom! Absalom*, perhaps the greatest American novel to
record the tragedies of race, in the poetic, moving, and terrifying description of the destruction of a dynasty, creates a symbolic way to understand
the tragedy of a nation.

Oprah, in the matter of family, color, and other issues, came to understand and forgive much that embittered her in earlier years. Time helped
to distance her from bitterness toward Vernita, whom she saw as an angry,
hostile parent, a woman with no love to spare for Oprah. The problems
Vernita faced as a single mother in bringing up three illegitimate children
on a minimal income, in tiny quarters, seem overwhelming to any on-
looker. Yet, surprisingly, she took much pride in her appearance, and even

during the periods when the family was on welfare, she saw to it that the children, like herself, were nicely dressed. Although some black women were able to improve their lives before the civil rights movement of the sixties, Vernita, with no training or education, could expect nothing more or better than she had and survival was a constant struggle.

Only her daughter Oprah's success and generosity years later as an entertainer improved Vernita's life. The less-favored child gave money to both siblings and her mother, as well as homes to her mother, sister, and father. Although her father, by far the better parent, wanted nothing except tires for an old truck, Oprah surprised him with an expensive Mercedes. Oprah has recounted in interviews that her half sister, Patricia Lloyd, was never satisfied by anything Oprah gave her and betrayed Oprah's intimate secrets to the newspapers and contradicted much that Oprah had previously said. It took several years for Oprah to forgive her. They were never close, nor has Oprah said that she feels much affection or obligation to any other family member except Vernon Winfrey. Yet she gave money to them, still. After failed attempts to get Jeffrey, her brother, to change his life and take responsibility for his actions, Oprah refused to help him financially, although without his knowing it, she provided extra money for him through Vernita. Filled with envy and bitterness, he accused her of ignoring him while helping an associate of hers, Billy Rizzo, who was dying from AIDS, the same illness from which Jeffrey died at age 29 in January 1989. Like Jeffrey, Patricia had a drug addiction, and her cocaine habit killed her at the age of 43 in February 2003.

Some of Oprah's own anger toward family members after she'd achieved fame and fortune, resulted from the expectations of relatives and their friends that she would help them monetarily, combined with the fact that they, like her sister and brother, did nothing to help themselves. Oprah has repeatedly stressed the admirability of self-help and responsibility, and though she has said little about her siblings' lack of initiative for changing their lives, she has little pity for such a weakness. Some biographers have claimed that Oprah holds back nothing about her life, but writer Barbara Grizzutti Harrison notes that Oprah does skirt issues having to do with her siblings.

The ghetto world of her mother offered few examples of betterment. Although Vernita had started out as a boarder and eventually had a two-bedroom apartment, her three children shared one of the bedrooms. Thus the living conditions were much worse for Oprah than they had been on Grandmother Lee's farm. Vernita's hopes for marriages brought disappointments in her personal life that were and are not uncommon, something Oprah learned to understand but which were beyond her comprehension when she was a child. Men came and went, even though Vernita had a relationship for several years with the man who fathered her son. She wanted and expected her children to follow rules about sexual behavior, yet she was no exemplar of what she advocated.

Experience in the larger world brought the mature Oprah into contact with many poor young black women whose lives resemble Vernita's. If Oprah had remained with her mother, the direction of her own life might well have been similar to Vernita's in spite of the fact that Oprah was an extremely bright child. For a time it seemed as though her future would be as bleak as that of many young ghetto black girls and women.

When Oprah was eight and had reached the end of her first term in the Milwaukee schools, Vernita, who was struggling financially, sent her to her father and stepmother in Nashville, to an environment completely opposite from the one she'd been living in. Her father, an industrious, hardworking man with a regular income, owned a barber shop and a small adjacent grocery store. This grocery store was where Oprah first had a job, though it was a job she has said she despised. An upstanding person, Winfrey later in life became a member of the city council. By any measurement he could provide a better milieu than Vernita could for their daughter. The Winfreys had a home in an established black, middle-class community, totally different from the poor, run-down Milwaukee area where Vernita lived. Because Vernon and his wife Zelma had no children of their own, they wanted to raise Oprah themselves. Strongly religious, Vernon Winfrey, a deacon, was very active in his church, Faith United, and saw to it, as Grandmother Lee had, that Oprah attended all services and youth-oriented activities. The Winfrey home was rigorously run, a place where learning for a child was central, and Zelma, known as a "strict disciplinarian," required Oprah to read a certain number of books on a regular basis, write, learn math, and develop a strong vocabulary.

Vernon and Zelma sent her to East Wharton Elementary School in Nashville. Encouraged by a fourth-grade teacher named Mrs. Duncan, whom she still remembers with deep affection, the child flourished. Over the years Oprah has frequently spoken lovingly of Mrs. Duncan, who inspired her so much that for a time she wanted to become a teacher also. In middle age, Oprah achieved that particular ambition, teaching for 10 weeks a course called "The Dynamics of Leadership" with her boyfriend, Stedman Graham, at Northwestern University's J. L. Kellogg School of Management. The course, which was open to 100 second-year graduate students was described as an official, for-credit course. In 2001 an undergraduate course *about* Oprah was offered. Its description in the catalog, referring to its subject matter as "Oprah the Tycoon," was Oprah's most recent teaching venture. The course, History 298, was offered at the Urbana-Champaign campus of the University of Illinois.

The memory of Mrs. Duncan always had a favored place in Oprah's heart. Because of Mrs. Duncan, Oprah has said that she believes strongly in the influence of teachers on the lives of children. However, in spite of Mrs. Duncan's affection for Oprah, the other children in her class were hostile, much as the children had been when she lived with her grandmother because she preached to them. They disliked her and thought she was crazy. Nevertheless, influenced by strong faith and the moral atmosphere of Vernon Winfrey's home, Oprah decided she'd become a missionary when she grew up and she even collected money for the poor of Costa Rica. Although she never became a missionary, the desire to help others in need became part of her own ethical fiber.

All of the future promise of the Winfrey household seemed to dissipate for Oprah when she was nine; in the summer of 1963, Oprah's mother, expecting to be married and hoping to have a real family life, insisted on her return to Wisconsin. Vernon Winfrey wasn't happy about having his daughter go back to the environment of Vernita's household. Oprah experienced regression into the overcrowded, unsupervised, undisciplined life she'd led before, only worse. She soon became the frequent object of sexual abuse. After first being raped by a cousin at an uncle's house when she was nine, over the next five years she experienced molestation that she has described as unending and persistent until she went to live again in her father's home. She was abused by numerous men, among them other relatives and her mother's boyfriends. When she was first raped by her cousin, she says, she didn't understand what had happened, particularly when the cousin convinced her not to tell by bribing her with an ice cream cone and a trip to a local zoo.

Although she kept the violations a "big, looming, dark secret" for more than 12 years, Oprah has said that she always believed that her mother knew about them and had failed to protect her. Also, like many other rape victims and abused children, she blamed herself for the terrible things that had happened to her, and she maintained her silence. She has said she thought of herself as a bad girl, and only when she reached her thirties and forties did she give up the belief that the sexual abuses had been her fault. When at the age of 24, she finally told her mother and other members of the family about the abuse, nobody would accept what she said.

Her mother's refusal to discuss the matter was so traumatic that Oprah "never brought it up again" with her. Nevertheless, the matter of her abuse became a public confession for Oprah on her television program when a woman, Trudy Chase, appeared on the show and spoke of the suffering she had experienced as a child as a result of sexual abuse. The identification for Oprah was so intense that all her efforts at concealment over the years slipped away in the shared moments of suffering with her guest. But she says that it has taken her a very long time to understand the anger and rebellion that came about from the destructive assaults she'd suffered. She needed and wanted affection that she couldn't get at home from her mother and siblings, and her feelings made her vulnerable to sexual predators. This pattern would repeat itself even after many years, something other women in similar circumstances have endured.

Almost three decades after the abuse first occurred, when Oprah had become an internationally famous entertainer on television and in film, she chose to use her celebrity as a means of speaking out against the terrors of child abuse and the secrecy that had always surrounded it. In 1992, she introduced a documentary titled *Scared Silent*, telling the audience about her own harsh childhood experiences of rape and molestation by male relatives and family friends. Urging both children and adults to watch the documentary, to talk about the issues, and to seek help, she appeared on a number of morning television programs including the *Today Show*, *This Morning*, and *Good Morning America*. Abuse, she stressed, on those programs and elsewhere, is not limited to any one class, or race, or economic level.

Her concern for other problems in the lives of children was expanded professionally the following year, 1993, in several ways. Her distress about the tragic results to children from the availability of handguns became the source of several "Child Alert" programs. Probably better known is *There Are No Children Here*, a combination fiction and documentary called "a true-life drama." In the picture Oprah plays a black "Everywoman." Although the film specifically focuses on blacks, when Oprah uses the term "Everywoman" to define herself, in life, as she presents her talk show and speaks with interviewees, she does not limit her scope to any race or color. She says that she believes a great many of her experiences to be the same as those of *every* woman. In the film her role is that of an African American mother attempting, in the midst of dire poverty and social ills, to raise her family and keep them together. The family, in addition to the central figure of the mother, consists of a grandmother played by Oprah's friend Maya Angelou, an undependable husband/father, and three sons: one already lost to the prison system, one "in the undecided column," and the youngest, for whom there is also still hope. The setting was the Henry Horner public housing project in Chicago, a place that had caught Oprah's attention for a long period of time as she drove past it on her way to work.

Talking about her experience of filming the project, Oprah said that she gained knowledge and insight into not only people's needs but also the longings and dreams for their lives that everyone harbors; with the recognition that she is "everywoman," came the understanding every human being goes through some basic human circumstances. Living in a project doesn't alter such emotions as joy, sorrow, and disappointment. But poverty and deprivation can shape existence. In an attempt to help some of the children she met while working on the film, Oprah donated to a scholarship fund all of the $500,000 salary she was paid, money that also was matched by ABC. She went even further than that by helping one particular family. She sent the 12-year-old child to private school and saw to it that the mother got psychological guidance, and that she and her older son found jobs. Oprah even sought to motivate all the other children who had been part of the film to improve their grades; she promised them a trip to Disneyland if they earned all As on their report cards.

Her philosophy of personal responsibility and self-help, as well as her belief in the vital role of education, is played out in practical ways, again and again, in situations such as these described above. In talks, interviews, on her television show, and in her magazine O, which she started in 2000 with the partnership of the Hearst Company, she emphasizes the possibility of change. Where once she wanted to keep many experiences private, now she appears more open, although some interviewers have said that she is carefully selective. But Oprah herself asserts that sharing the truth with others is freeing and uplifting. Nobody should allow the past to define him or her, and she points to her own life as validation of that view.

Her own early years taught her much of this philosophy, even though she could not have had any idea of the direction her life would take. In a lengthy interview she gave to Newsweek reporter Lynette Clemetson, she insists that the efforts and rewards of her life were never calculated. But she has also said that all the different experiences of her childhood and youth have given her greater understanding of the problems others must deal with. When she lived with her mother for the second time, in spite of finding herself in more and more emotional and physical trouble, she did very well at the Lincoln Middle School, located in the inner city, the poor section of Milwaukee. Clever and talented, a good student as well as an ardent reader even then, Oprah was able, with help from a teacher, to obtain a scholarship in 1968 to Nicolet, a private, newly integrated Milwaukee high school. Because she lived 20 miles from the school, she had to take three buses to get there, often riding with her mother and the other maids on their way to work.

Each trip brought a change of landscape, taking her from the dilapidated, rundown area that was her home to a neighborhood of houses surrounded by greenery, lawns and trees, and flowers. It was an entrance into another world, and she was an outsider, a penniless black child, spending days with rich white children who often invited her to their homes after school. She longed for everything these girls had, normal families, elegant clothing, spending money, pets. In their houses the children would introduce her to their black maids as if all black people should know each other, and made the same assumption about Oprah's supposed familiarity with black entertainers. For Oprah, these memories still linger. With a certain wry humor on her television show, she points out that some white people imagine many untrue things about blacks.

The year that Oprah attended Nicolet High is also a time that will long be remembered in history. In 1968 both Martin Luther King and Robert Kennedy were assassinated. From the period of Oprah's birth through the decade of the sixties, upheaval was prevalent: the year she was born, 1954, the U.S. Supreme Court ruled that segregation in public schools was unconstitutional, although Mississippi didn't have racial integration of its public schools until 1964. Violence was "endemic to Mississippi," an extremism that "burst into the national awareness in the summer of 1955," the year after Oprah's birth. That summer in Mississippi white men murdered a 14-year-old black boy named Emmett Till, who allegedly had whistled at a white woman. Till's murder became an important part of civil rights legendry, along with the refusal by Rosa Parks, a black woman in Montgomery Alabama, to follow the custom of giving up her seat to a white person and sit in the back of a bus. Parks's behavior landed her in jail, an act that brought about the Montgomery boycott of bus transportation and led to more legal changes. Parks's name has long been associated with the Court's action against segregation in transportation. Oprah paid homage to Parks when she included her as an honored guest at a screening of *Beloved*, held at Marianne Williamson's Church of Today.

Parks was not the first black woman who attempted to alter American laws and bring about civil rights. A forerunner of Parks was Ida B. Wells, born a slave in 1862, in Oprah's home state of Mississippi. Like the later Parks, Wells refused to be segregated. While aboard a train she was told to exchange her seat in a ladies' railroad car for one in a car set aside for black people. When she would not comply, she was removed from the train. Wells brought a suit against the railroad, a suit that she won, but the decision was later reversed by the Supreme Court of Tennessee. While her win was surprising even in the post–Civil War South, the reversal was not. Undaunted by defeat, Wells spent much of her life in efforts, usually unsuccessful, to improve the lot of black people. After becoming a part owner and writer for a Memphis newspaper, she was determined to leave the South after the newspaper office was destroyed by white men in retaliation for her antilynching columns. Alienated from the South but not from the cause of civil rights, she moved to Chicago generations before Richard Wright or the birth of Oprah. In Chicago Wells founded the first African American civic group for women, and also became the first president of the Negro Fellowship League and chairman of the Equal Rights League of Chicago. Her greatest and most lasting accomplishment came in 1909, when she helped found the oldest and probably the best-known national civil rights organization in the United States, the one that eventually became the NAACP, the National Association for the Advancement of Colored People.

Oprah is captivated by the history and powerful heritage left by a few black women. The year she reached the age of six (1962), and moved from Mississippi to Milwaukee, was the historic time that a black student, James Meredith, had to be enrolled by force in Oxford, at the University of Mississippi. Of course, she holds no individual knowledge of any of the political events that happened during the early years of her childhood or half a century before her birth, and she was only a small child when the first civil rights bills for blacks since Reconstruction in the nineteenth century were passed. In spite of, or because of these and other momentous changes, for a number of years unrest was prevalent with sit-ins, riots, civil rights marches, and even murders that led to the frequent calling up of federal troops. This was the period of Oprah's adolescence and early adulthood, and she, typical of other adolescents, was more concerned with her familiar world than the political situation around her.

It isn't surprising, given that Oprah was only a teenager in the sixties, that she has been detached from politics, in her home state or elsewhere. Apparently, though, her neutrality toward politics has not changed. Neither someone to carry a banner nor dress like a woman from Africa, she has her own original concept of ways to change society. She does not speak for any political party, although her home state, Mississippi, was and remains a Democratic state. Every governor since 1874 has been a Democrat, except for two. Yet the two current state senators are Republicans:

Thad Cochran has held office since 1979, and Trent Lott was reelected in 2000 along with Republican President George W. Bush. In 1969, Charles Evers, the first black mayor of Fayette since Reconstruction, was elected. A mature Oprah, though, philanthropic as she is, continues to keep her distance and never involves herself in any state or federal politics. On her television show she has interviewed Democratic and Republican presidents and their first ladies and appeared with them on other occasions that involved matters of national interest. She made one exception to her usual neutral stance when she invited her friends Maria Shriver and Arnold Schwarzenegger, who was a candidate for governor in California, to appear on her program. Nevertheless, she is independent enough to turn down requests to appear with heads of state. In 2002 she refused an invitation from President George Bush to join a group of officials on a trip to tour Afghanistan schools; Oprah responded "no," saying that she was too much involved with earlier commitments. That unguarded statement provided the media with the chance for some Oprah bashing by people who regarded her response as a political snub of the administration.

Because of her celebrity she often is asked, both seriously and humorously, whether she might consider running for some political office; she always answers with an emphatic "no." Even though some people see her as a political figure, throughout her adult years Oprah's concern has not been for political movements but for the rights of all women everywhere, as well as other individuals whose lives she celebrates. Furthermore, apart from politics, she has shown a lifelong desire to help those in need, overlooked, or discriminated against.

Part of her outlook mirrors activist Jesse Jackson's: excellence is the best barrier to both sexism and racism. Responsibility for our lives belongs to each of us; furthermore, both Jackson and Oprah have said that the path to freedom is through education. Above all else, education alters everything. Oprah is even more passionate about education for women, remembering the limits of Vernita's life and those of others like her. With heartfelt admiration for Oprah, Jackson remarks about the enormity of her contribution to transforming the social structure, an observation echoed hyperbolically in Vanity Fair magazine, characterizing her influence as greater than almost anyone on the planet except for the Pope. And, the news magazine, Time, in 1998 listed her as one of the twentieth-century's "Most Influential People." The magazine repeated that listing for the twenty-first century, in 2004.

Jackson, on a personal note, describes Oprah in the same way she depicts her cherished friend Quincy Jones, as a person who lights up the dark places. Year after year, in addition to categorizing her as a prominent figure, polls also have listed her as one of the most admired women in America, along with first ladies, a woman senator (Hillary Rodham Clinton), and a former British prime minister (Lady Margaret Thatcher). Oprah's style of participation in the lives of the underprivileged and African Americans, however, in the main does not resemble Jackson's. While Oprah's beneficence may be directed primarily toward blacks, it isn't closed to others. After all, most of her female television audience at home and abroad, much of her staff, and many of her friends are white. Thus, when Jackson, in March 1996, protested the Academy Awards because of the lack of black nominees—only one black person among 166 nominees—it isn't surprising that Oprah, Whoopi Goldberg, and Quincy Jones criticized his action: Jones, not incidentally, was the producer of the awards show.

Oprah's belief in individual accountability is much more pronounced than any advocacy for broader, societal changes, though the exceptions are her calls for stricter gun laws, punishment for those who commit sex crimes against children, and the need for education. This emphasis on the individual has at various times led to critics' calling her conservative and capitalistic. Nevertheless, her great commitment to the life-transforming value of education may be seen in many areas. Her personal views become evident in, for example, the 10 ongoing scholarships she established in her father's name at her alma mater, Tennessee State University, after she became a television star. She continues to give major sums of money to colleges and universities, large and small. Recently, Cuyahoga Community College, in Cleveland, was attempting to raise $600,000 for scholarships when Winfrey gave a keynote speech there in late 2002. She learned that the admissions office was turning away students from the school because there wasn't enough money available for scholarships, and in a typical gesture, she made the offer to help. Oprah's matching gift to Cuyahoga was in recognition of the importance of both her own spiritual and educational beginnings. Her extremely generous gift of $5 million to the black college Morehouse—not the first, she'd given the college $1 million previously and remains the school's top donor—is typical of her public spiritedness. She has been very liberal in her donations to many other schools and colleges. However, she hasn't limited her educational concerns to the United States; she has also taken an active philanthropic role in providing funds for international schools. In fact, when she is asked about her plans for after she leaves her show, she mentions, among other activities, her wish to become more involved with education in Africa, something she has already begun to do in building schools for girls. In recent years she has spoken of her desire to be a constructive force in the lives of those who need it. However, in spite of the fact that she regards herself as a nurturer, she has said again and again that she never felt the desire for motherhood. When asked, as she frequently is, whether she ever wanted to be a mother she answers in the negative, making the point that she never had a role model for motherhood in Vernita.

An admiring world forgets or doesn't know the damaged, rebellious girl she was, light ages away from the exquisitely coiffed and dressed woman she became. At 14, Oprah's personal problems caught up with her. One sexual episode followed another, including an instance with her father's brother, Trent, another abusive situation she never spoke about until years later, and even then her father found the knowledge almost impossible to accept. Today, she tells girls and women that they must not keep such things to themselves, that the burden of abuse cannot be tolerated. She teaches that in order to become responsible for one's own life, one has to tell the truth about an abusive situation again and again, until someone listens. This lesson results from something she did not do as a child herself.

Oprah kept secret from her mother the frequent, ongoing attacks by men who came and went in their home. Vernita, finding it impossible to control her daughter, tried various avenues unsuccessfully, including an attempt to place the girl in a home for wayward children. Finally Vernon agreed to take Oprah back to live with him and Zelma. Neither he nor Vernita knew at the time that the teenage girl was pregnant because, like her mother 14 years earlier, she was extremely successful at concealing her condition. Only when she was in her seventh month did she tell her father the truth. Today she recognizes him as a "proud and honorable man," the person who saved her life, that is, the one who saw to it that she became more than an unwed mother. Without the influence of Vernon Winfrey throughout her adolescent years, she could not have achieved her later success. Oprah recalls his strength as he considered the choices that existed in her situation and then reached the decision to allow her to have the baby. However, two weeks after the premature infant boy's birth, he died. What the 14-year-old Oprah's feelings were at the time may not be precisely what the middle-aged woman describes as an "opportunity" rather than a loss, the opportunity presented was for a choice of her future. Yet there is no question that the path she would have had to take would have no resemblance to the one she had been on. She freely admits she has no idea of what her life might have been or what sort of mother she would have become. There are many examples of teenagers whose futures have been defined by the boundaries of motherhood, and in 1968 a pregnant black girl of 14 would have had few prospects or hope.

Freed of the oppressions of life in Vernita's home and of teenage motherhood, Oprah began to show signs of promise, although surely nobody in those days could have predicted her later accomplishments. In spite of the fact that she had no idea what the future would bring, she has said that she remembers telling her father, when she was still a youngster, that one day she'd be famous. After moving in with the Winfreys once more, she had to follow their strict rules. Vernon Winfrey was uncompromising about grades, demanding she earn As. Cs, he told his daughter, were not acceptable for one who has the capacity to excel. Further, he didn't agree that she should be rewarded for her achievements, even with an ice cream cone, because he simply expected her to be the best. Zelma, his wife, again required Oprah to do all the things necessary to become an outstanding student.

When she was about 15, Oprah began to keep her journal and has continued it ever since then. Now when she rereads its entries from her teen years, she sees page after page filled with typical kinds of entries: problems with boys; trivial complaints about her father's dos and don'ts—all the same complaints as those of most American teenage girls. Nonetheless, after entering Nashville's East High School, she became very active in her class; soon she was chosen as vice president of her class, president of the student council, drama club, and National Forensics League. Voted "most popular" girl in her senior year, she also was chosen for membership in the honor society. In 1971, during the Nixon administration, when two students from each state and from foreign countries were chosen to attend a White House Conference on Youth, Oprah was one of Tennessee's representatives.

Shortly after that she was interviewed at a small Nashville radio station, WVOL, an event that led the way to her later career. The station, white-owned but black-operated and with a primarily black audience, wanted somebody to represent them in the contest for Miss Fire Prevention. Oprah was recommended by John Heidelberg, who all these years later still recalls how much he was impressed both by her articulateness and ease before a camera. He was the person who had interviewed her when she searched for supporters for a March of Dimes Walkathon. The Miss Fire Prevention competition was actually a beauty contest, in which every girl except Oprah was white, and she has said, with characteristic humor, that all of the girls were redheads. Relaxed because she was certain she had no chance at winning, but proud and delighted with her new evening gown, she answered the two test questions with the lightheartedness that later characterized her. First asked what she'd do with the money if she won, she told the judges she'd be a "spending fool." And when asked about her wishes for a future career, she chose something out of the ordinary for that day and time: it was to be a journalist in the broadcasting industry. Other contestants had given expected, typical answers, so Oprah won, becoming the first black girl to be named Miss Fire Prevention. Following her unanticipated success, she became the first Miss Black Nashville in a pageant; later, in another pageant she was named Miss Black Tennessee, and, following that, she even won a trip to Hollywood where she participated in, though she didn't win, a Miss Black America contest. Those were only the beginning of honors that were to come her way throughout the decades.

In 1971, after graduating from high school, she went on to Tennessee State University with a scholarship paid for by an Elks lodge where she won a contest. She majored in speech and language arts, although she was uncertain about her future plans. Yet, the path to a career was opening up, beginning with that interview she'd had in her senior year in high school, after she was chosen as Miss Fire Prevention. She was offered a job with the radio station WVOL, reading the news. Characteristic of Oprah's outgoing personality, just for fun while at the station, she'd read some of the news copy. As a result of the favorable impression she'd made with her voice and poise, when the station needed somebody for the job, the people there, particularly John Heidelberg, remembered her. Naive and somewhat unworldly, she knew little about media. Of course, it didn't occur to her that the opportunity and exposure through reading the news would pave the way to a future career and international fame. She was going to turn down the offer, fearful the job might interfere with school work, but her father encouraged her to take it. Although he hadn't been too enthusiastic about her choice of a major, he was pleased by the opportunities that were coming her way. Doing the weekend news, and later occasional broadcasts during the week, she worked her way up from no pay to $100 a week, a large sum of money in those years.

Later, while in college, she was given an even more prestigious opportunity with a larger radio station, WLAC, and not long after that, at the age of 19, she moved to its television channel, WLAC-TV, where she became a reporter and coanchorperson, the first woman as well as the first black person to hold that position. Though still reluctant about accepting such an offer, she was persuaded to do so by Professor William Cox, who oversaw her major courses. He pointed out that the job was in the area of work for which she had been preparing. Furthermore, her father, who supervised almost everything she did, agreed with her professor. In later years, when questioned whether she'd seen herself as a so-called token for the job, she has made light of it, yet at the same time acknowledging the reality, saying she had been a very happy token. Speaking of the matter at another time, she also said pointedly that she was a paid token. Oprah has never shown any regrets, surely not publicly, about accepting opportunities of that sort. The seventies were a changing period in America, when doors previously closed to women and people of color were slowly opening as a result of civil rights laws.

Oprah's world was expanding, not only with a job but also through opportunities to do some acting in college and singing with "Sweet Honey in the Rock," an all-female a cappella group in Nashville. The group describes itself as singing of "struggle, perseverance, and triumph," celebrating life "deeply rooted in the African American experience." Naturally, Oprah was attracted to it, and apparently so were its audiences—three decades later, the group still sings in many parts of the South.

But after a time, the restrictions of life at home—with her stern father's rules, which included a curfew, as well as the difficulties of meshing college studies and work—led to a life-altering decision on her part. She left college without her degree, moving on to another job in the media, becoming a reporter and coanchor of evening news at a Baltimore, Maryland, station. Although several biographies state that Oprah graduated from college in 1976, the fact is that she did not, and the actual situation is somewhat cloudy. One version is that she received an honorary degree years later. Another is that Tennessee State University awarded her a bachelor of arts degree in 1987. Still another is that she was asked by the university in 1987 to give the commencement address, but she refused to do it until she had finished her courses for credit and obtained her degree.

Whatever the actual facts are, she does have a degree from Tennessee State. Furthermore, like her friend and mentor, Maya Angelou, Oprah since 2002 may be addressed as "doctor." Princeton University awarded honorary degrees to Oprah and a number of other people famous in various fields: from baseball (Cal Rifken, Jr.) to medicine (Anthony Fauci) to history (Colin Lucas and Bernard Lewis) to religion (James Forbes, Jr.) to playwriting (Emily Mann). Oprah's is an honorary doctorate of fine arts. At the same ceremony, another talk host, Terry Gross, of the National Public Radio show *Fresh Air*, was also granted an honorary doctor of humanities degree.

Not long after that, another recognition came to Oprah when she was the chosen recipient of the sixth Marian Anderson Award. Recipients generally donate the prize of $100,000 to a favorite charity. Many who remember the opera star's soul-stirring contralto voice forget that she lived in a period when segregation kept her from many of the venues open to famous singers today. After a board's scandalous recall of an invitation to her to sing at Constitution Hall, Anderson was then invited to the White House, where she became the first black singer to perform. Because Anderson, a native of Philadelphia, broke through one of the most important barriers in Jim Crowism, her home state pays homage to her memory, for that and other significant actions.

Philadelphia Mayor John Street, speaking of the 2003 choice of Oprah for the Anderson award, took note of Oprah's work in many social programs, as well as her generosity to schools at home and in South Africa; he also pointed to the importance of her television shows that focus on individual self-help. Oprah, says the mayor, serves as "a national mentor." Following the mayor's announcement, Pamela Crowley, the chairman of the award's board of directors and senior vice president for public affairs for Citizens Bank in Philadelphia, spoke. She compared Oprah to Marian Anderson, calling attention to the similarities in their characters; both women, she emphasized, achieved their place in the world through their own abilities and efforts. Several years earlier, Oprah received the Horatio Alger Award from the association that annually honors those who have triumphed over adversity with their considerable achievements. Almost everyone who mentions Oprah speaks with awe of her astonishing rise from annihilating poverty to her place on the world's stage.

Many experiences in Oprah's younger years were similar to those of other black women of her age. One such event she recalls happened when she was chosen to participate in another black college contest to be held outside of Nashville. There, in Chicago, housed in a rundown motel in a high-crime area on the South Side, the young college participants were outraged by the conditions they found. However, in what was to become typical of the future star, Oprah disregarded the adverse circumstances, becoming the second-place winner in the contest with her reading of a passage from Ntozake Shange's *For Colored Girls Who Have Contemplated Suicide when the Rainbow Is Enuf,* a play assigned in many English classes throughout the country.

Could anyone knowing her early life have imagined the heights to which she would rise, that in 1996 she would receive the most notable

honor in broadcasting, the George Foster Peabody Individual Achievement Award, and a few years after that, in 2002, she would be the first recipient of the Bob Hope Humanitarian Award? Decades earlier, when
Oprah left Nashville to try her wings elsewhere, she was 22, young and
unsophisticated in various ways, only at the beginning of the road that
would eventually take her to stardom. Going from relatively small
Nashville to Baltimore, the tenth-largest city in the country, was not an
easy transition for a young woman. It took years for her to become the
equal of the assured, self-confident person she praises in Maya Angelou's
poem, "Phenomenal Woman," years to learn the "secret" of being herself:
neither "cute" nor slim as a "model," but someone both "cool" and fiery,
filled with the joy of life and being a woman. Starting out, she didn't do
well in her new job as the anchor of the six o'clock evening news on Baltimore's station, WJZ-TV, the largest station in the city. She was ill at
ease, and her unworldly background led to embarrassing gaffes. It became
apparent very quickly that Oprah wasn't meant to be a newswoman. Her
strength then, as now, was her rapport with people, not her ability to
cover the news. Far too emotional to be a reporter, she would get carried
away and react to the human aspects of all situations. Although she freely
admits her lack of qualifications for journalism, years later—in 2000—she
joined the ranks of magazine owners and writers when the highly successful magazine O was launched.

When her career was really in its infancy, though, both her reportorial
mode and her appearance troubled the producers. In an attempt to alter
her looks, they sent her to New York for a so-called makeover. A special
hair treatment and permanent caused most of her hair to fall out, with the
result that she lost her job as well as her hair. She was demoted from her
6 P.M. anchor position, but luckily a new station manager who liked
Oprah's style found a slot for her with a male cohost, Richard Sher, on a
morning program called People Are Talking. Even though the show proved
to be quite popular, Oprah didn't particularly like working with another
host. However, because she enjoyed doing a talk show, something she always has described as being natural as breathing, she stayed with the job
for several years.

Surprisingly, with the large black population of Baltimore and the
comfortable numbers of viewers in that city, the program had a smaller
viewing audience there than in 12 other cities. However, in Baltimore itself, her program did have a higher rating than the leading national talk
show, Donahue, a statistic that was to help her find another job. Restless
and unhappy in her personal life, and tired of what she'd been doing for

six years, she began to look elsewhere for work. With the help of a resume expert, and her own efforts as well as those of an ambitious producer friend, in 1984, at the age of 30, Oprah relocated to the city she has referred to as "a more polished New York," Chicago, which had the third largest television market in the country. There she has remained for more than two decades. When she first became host, though, the show she took over was low in the ratings. Nervous about the kind of competition she faced, she voiced those feelings to station manager Dennis Swanson, whose response was to be herself since there was no way she could be Phil Donahue. Nevertheless, in that different kind of environment for Oprah, within months, the program she hosted, AM Chicago, gained one of the highest talk show ratings and soon was the most popular talk show on the air. With a starting salary of $225,000, she considered herself unbelievably rich.

Only two years after her move to Chicago, her show was syndicated, and, in a sense, a star was born, the star of what became known then as The Oprah Winfrey Show. When the show went national in 1986, 32-year-old Oprah celebrated Thanksgiving with Vernon and Zelma Winfrey; the three of them took a triumphal trip back to Mississippi, where they revisited family and friends and old haunts from Oprah's childhood. Her grandmother's house is now gone, but the street alongside the property is known as "Oprah Winfrey Road." In Kosciusko Oprah's celebrity is as great or perhaps greater than in other parts of the country. Nashville, somewhat later, also paid tribute to Oprah—and her father's role in her life—by naming the street on which Vernon Winfrey's Beauty and Barber shop is located "Vernon Winfrey Avenue."

Only a year after that vacation, in 1987, Oprah was awarded an Emmy for daytime television, the first of the more than 30 that would follow over the years until at last she was given a lifetime award.

The syndication of her show was the most significant step to stardom, because it made her a national and soon thereafter an international figure. Renaming the program as The Oprah Winfrey Show was the act of the King Brothers Corporation, a company owned by two very well-known distributors who had purchased the show in September 1986. They soon saw to it that the program was on 137 stations nationwide. Roger, known as a so-called high flyer and big spender, and by far the more daring and flamboyant of the brothers, predicated accurately that syndication would make Oprah rich. However, Oprah, herself has said that the phenomenal success of the program came about from its being on the air at the same time throughout the country, and although the program is shown during the daylight hours, she considers it to be, as do some critics, a prime-time show.

Always giving credit to the Kings for the major role they've played in her career, she has said that without them she wouldn't have achieved her enormous following. Over the years the Kings have remained the sole distributors of her show, although Oprah owns and controls it through her company. Even after the CBS Corporation in 1999 bought the television syndicate company, King World Productions, for $2.5 billion, King World continues to hold the right to sell shows to rival networks. Oprah's show continues to bring in large sums of money; estimates of the number of weekly watchers for Oprah's show have varied greatly, ranging from 15 million to more than twice that number. The total depends on whether the count is limited to the United States or includes some or all of the foreign viewers. By the end of the twentieth century Oprah's show earned approximately 40 percent of the revenues of King World, a company of which she now is a major stockholder.

Frequently referred to as "the boys," the King Brothers, Roger and Michael, are white, middle-aged men, part of a family of six brothers who inherited a struggling syndicate business when their father, Charlie King, died. Roger and Michael were able to turn the marginal business into a multimillion-dollar company that, in turn, made huge amounts of money for the television programs they represented, so that they became the powerhouse dealers of television programs. Although most of their clients have been very successful game shows, Oprah is the star in their crown. Periodically, whenever there is speculation about Oprah's plans to retire, she signs a new contract with the Kings. The recent announcement that she "has had second thoughts about retiring" was no surprise. By May of 2003 she told the public she was having too great a time to give up her work.

In spite of his extraordinary financial acumen, Roger King, the six foot four, two hundred pounder, is a rather surprising person to have business dealings with Oprah. He is a colorful figure who likes to gamble and spend extravagantly. Nonetheless, without the Kings, Oprah might never have achieved the exposure she gets on television nor the vast sums of money she's acquired. The Kings are known to woo clients with gifts and trips and lavish spending. Oprah, like the other entertainers with whom the Kings deal, has been the recipient of some of their largesse.

Although when Oprah took on the Chicago program, Phil Donahue was the leader in the talk show business and people spoke of him as the "owner" of daytime television, Oprah toppled him. In spite of her having learned what to do by watching tapes of his shows in addition to those of Barbara Walters, and of being grateful to Donahue for paving the way, hers was a different kind of approach. Donahue, who is just as gracious about Oprah as she is about him, praises her ability to connect with her audience, pointing with admiration to the speed with which she gained huge markets: what took him a decade to do she accomplished in a single year, he tells interviewers, comparing her ascent to a skyrocket. Donahue left Chicago; although he denies leaving because of her competition, he did move his show to New York but was never able to regain his status in television and retired for a period of time. He attempted a comeback on MSNBC-TV in 2002–3; however, television critics had few kind words for him, and after six months, his newest program was dropped. Where Donahue was intense, Oprah was easy. Audience and guests responded to her, forming a loyal following that continues into the twenty-first century.

Within a few years of her move to Chicago, the illegitimate daughter of Vernita Lee and Vernon Winfrey became a millionaire, and, according to various reports, not only among the top ten but also the richest entertainer in the world; additionally *Forbes* listed her as being one of the wealthiest people in America, and in September 1993 tabulated her wealth as $98 million, higher than the $72 million of producer Steven Spielberg, who had given her the first of her movie roles. Her wealth is also more than the $66 million of Bill Cosby, comedian, television actor, and venerated friend of Oprah. Ten years later, 2003, when *Forbes* ranked the 100 richest people in the world, Oprah made the list as the first black American billionaire. Among a group of 222 Americans and 134 Europeans, Oprah's fortune of one billion dollars is not high on the register, but she was one of the three billionaires whose photos appear on the cover of the magazine. The others were the Walton heirs, the family of Sam Walton, founder of Wal-Mart stores; and Bill Gates, star of the computer industry, cofounder and chairman of Microsoft and the world's richest man.

By 1986 Oprah had earned enough money to buy what most Chicagoans dream of, a penthouse condominium on the lakefront, with a view from the fifty-seventh floor not only of the lake but also of the city itself. The apartment contains everything anyone could dream of: crystal chandeliers—even in the walk-in closets that house the most exquisite designer clothing, the Valentinos, Ungaros, and Krizias. As a so-called luxury queen, Oprah enjoys spending on anything and everything that catches her eye, like highly expensive imported cotton T-shirts. She also enjoys giving to people who work with her—for example, fancy boots to 200 members of her staff—and gifting large amounts of money to friends.

The Chicago apartment also holds a wine cellar, as well as a marble tub with spigots made to resemble gold dolphins, a tub in which Oprah, known for her love of bubble bath, can soak. After the bath, Oprah, who calls herself "a homebody" can choose from a huge selection of elegant pajamas—dozens and dozens, she says. Her enjoyment of luxury also runs to a $100,000 BMW car.

Today she owns three other homes; her home in Rolling Prairie, Indiana, is a 160-acre farm with a 40-acre meadow designed by Washington landscape architect James van Sweden, and a $2-million house. Oprah loves dogs—and possesses several—the number has been given as nine— with her favorites being two cocker spaniels named Solomon and Sophie; she has a heated house for them. There are thoroughbred horses on the farm, and an additional feature is a helicopter pad. A famed architect, Bruce Gregg, designed the villa for her 85-acre ranch outside of Telluride, a Colorado ski area. The third house is a 42-acre, $50 million estate with a 23,000 square foot mansion in Montecito, California. Journalists have written that rumor suggests that Oprah paid for her California home with a personal check. She also owns several beachfront lots on the island of Maui in Hawaii. To get from one place to another easily, she bought a jet plane.

Oprah's growing wealth permitted her to make an even more important purchase. It came at the same time she joined the ranks of the most famous broadcasters—Walter Cronkite, David Brinkley, Barbara Walters, Ted Koppel, and others—as Broadcaster of the Year; she acquired ownership and control of the *Oprah Winfrey Show* from the Chicago ABC-TV station WLS and formed the company Harpo, which she will not allow to go public. Following that purchase, to house her new business, she bought an old building that had been a hockey rink. Taking great pleasure in the renovation, she turned it into multiple offices and production areas, as well as a spa and a gym where she works out. She personally selected almost everything from the large carpets and tile to the small doorknobs and doodads that went into remodeling.

Oprah is the first black woman to have her own studio and production company. Only two other American women have achieved that, and both were white: Mary Pickford and Lucille Ball. She is chairman and chief executive of the Harpo Entertainment Group that operates her show, develops various types of films, prime-time television specials, as well as children's specials, and home videos. By the year 2002 Harpo was estimated by *Fortune* magazine to be worth $575 million, with Oprah as owner of 90 percent of the stock.

Former entertainment lawyer, Jeff Jacobs, who had helped her originally set up the company, became president of Harpo a few years later and owner of 10 percent of its stock. Oprah has praised him as having both the foresight and imagination for the company, and although he calls her a "hands-on" person, as others do of her later endeavors on her magazine O, he is the person who carries out the running of the company. The writer of an article about Oprah's financial empire identifies Jacobs as "strategic advisor" and "combative deal maker," all of which translates into the term Oprah herself uses—"a piranha." Whatever the description, Jacobs played a major role in her financial success, not only as corporate president but also as a no-fee agent who negotiates her roles in movies and television. With both of them steering the company, by 1994, with 221 employees, of whom 68 percent were women, Harpo had grown so large that Oprah hired a chief operating officer, Tim Bennett, a television station executive whom she liked and knew well.

Oprah's desire to give back to others led to her creation of the "Angel Network" in 1997. She launched the organization to encourage philanthropy and volunteerism by people who have the means and/or energy to help those in need. With her desire to do good as a strong motivating force, she is like the missionary she once dreamed of becoming, to bring a message of goodness to others. But one person alone, even one very wealthy person, cannot help multitudes in material ways. Thus, the impulse behind the formation of the Angel Network is to inspire other fortunate people to return something to society, through good deeds, money, or both. From the beginning, participants in the network, working with another famous charitable group, Habitat for Humanity, have provided homes to thousands of families; funded college scholarships that allow needy and meritorious students to seek higher education; and given extremely large awards to people whose lives have been used in the service of others. The two earliest Angel programs are well known: the "Build an Oprah House," a joint effort with the Habitat for Humanity construction group; and "The World's Largest Piggy Bank," an appeal to collect money for underprivileged children.

In 1999 Oprah undertook still another business venture; as a cofounder with Geraldine Laybourne and Marcy Carsey, she bought 8 percent of a new cable company called Oxygen Media. One reason she bought into the company, she said, is always to have a voice, that is, a vehicle to express herself in a way that is different from other network programming. Oxygen Media is oriented toward women and topics that concern them, although on occasion the program subject matter has been directed to a wider audience. It is on for 24 hours a day, seven-days-a-week; however, the network hasn't achieved the hoped-for success. Even though it added a new chat show called *Oprah After the Show*, with working women in mind, the cable channel is said to be faltering, in part because it is available only to a limited number of people, fewer than half of the 105 million homes in the United States. Also, pollsters have said that the majority of women viewers would rather watch the Lifetime channel, known as the "Television for Women" channel.

Oprah could be a poster figure for the words in an advertisement, "You've come a long way, baby." No matter the barricades and hardships along the way, from the time she was a very young child—four or five—in the segregated state of Mississippi, where her grandparents had almost nothing, she has told interviewers that she had a sense that her life would be different, although she could not articulate her feelings. Four decades later, a middle-aged Oprah, remembering those childhood days and longings, talked to the spring 1997 graduating senior class at Wellesley College about the journey they would take into the future. Telling the young women about herself, she reminded them that life itself "is a journey" and listed a series of things that have been important to her. As she spoke of what she'd learned from her own pilgrimage, she exhorted the graduates to follow certain guidelines that have served her well along the way. She said that she had to discover who she was and who she was not and reminded each of them of the need to gain that kind of knowledge from their own experiences.

It took Oprah a long time and many so-called lessons to discover, as she said, that we can only be ourselves, not somebody else, no matter how admirable that somebody might be. When reminiscing about her beginnings, she made fun of her own early pretenses, her attempts to emulate celebrities she admires. To pretend to be someone other than who we are leads to disaster. Crediting Maya Angelou for helping her understand the principle of leading from truth, she urged her young Wellesley audience and others to do the same from the beginning, not after multiple disappointments. Living that way, Oprah maintains, is central to one's survival. So too is acceptance of our mistakes, but not acceptance alone: it is using all experiences to become wise, to grow beyond failures and move ahead.

In rereading the same journal she has kept for decades, she tells her listeners, she is able to trace her own personal growth from the days of adolescent silliness and immaturity to adult understanding of how to live each moment. In her speech, she urged the Wellesley graduating class, as she has exhorted viewers of her television show and readers of her magazine, to emulate her experience of keeping a journal. Not just an ordinary journal, it should be "a grateful journal," the kind of record that matters, because that type of narrative leads to focusing on plenitude rather than on lack. The "grateful" journal enriches life. Belief in possibility, in the abundance of the universe, becomes belief in what our individual lives can be.

Underscoring the spiritual side of Oprah is her own sense of connection to the so-called fountainhead, which to her is God, but she allows it may be called the life force, or "nature," or "Allah," or "the power." Whatever one calls that wellspring, it is the anchor for limitless achievements. Not feeling the necessity of organized religion, she doesn't limit faith to traditional modes. Confessing to not being much of a churchgoer, on occasion she does attend a service, generally at a south-side church in Chicago, Trinity United Church of Christ. But, characteristically, she puts no boundaries on the possibilities of anyone's life. Church, she has said, is within oneself. If a person is able to find the connection to a higher power, anything is attainable. Illustrating her sentiments with examples from her professional experiences, she advised her Wellesley audience to dream large because small dreams bring only small returns.

From the time Oprah realized she'd been given a second chance in life by her father, she has worked unceasingly, not only on her career but also to build an image outside the world of entertainment. Among the many important roles she has played, one of the most meaningful took place after the catastrophic events of September 2001, when as master of ceremonies, Oprah led an interfaith ceremony at Yankee Stadium in New York. Present for that occasion were people not only from the world of entertainment but from many other professions; religious and political leaders in addition to actors and singers all joined together to show the country and the world the unity of Americans in the aftermath of national tragedy.

All Americans have experienced that tragedy as a group, but several thousand have felt the tragedy of personal loss. Through talks, music, and writing, Oprah addresses the specificity of loss and despair, as well as other wrenching issues of life, probing the dark places and the light of possibility. In her magazine, in column after column entitled "What I Know for Sure," she writes of sadness and joy, of deprivation and fulfillment, of ordinariness and miracles, of soup and sunsets. All of these, she declares, are part of life's journey, and surely of hers. But each life creates its own path, although she has said she strongly believes that everything along the way happens for a reason and can add up to wholeness if we will it. Oprah's counsel for following our own path tells us we are responsible for our own happiness: we must give love first to ourselves and then to others.

Still, as she points to her own life as an example of possibility, she knows, even as she gives her inspirational talks, that few people, female or male, will ever come near the eminence she has reached.

Chapter 3

TELEVISIONLAND

When Howard Kurtz, a reporter for the *Washington Post* and host of an evening news discussion program on CNN, wrote the book *Hot Air: All Talk All the Time*, he listed names of performers he labeled "high priests of talk." All are familiar to any television or radio listener or even to people who are neither but know them just from general conversations held over the years. Of the seven Kurtz chooses from both daytime and nighttime talk shows—King, McLaughlin, Limbaugh, Imus, Donahue, Winfrey, and Koppel—Oprah is the only woman. As number six in Kurtz's group, she isn't the lead figure. However, no matter where her name appears in lists of television figures, her fans make up either the first or second largest audience of daytime television watchers/listeners. Journalists have designated Oprah "Queen of Daytime Television" because by the mid-nineties, a larger number of women opted to watch her programs instead of any other offering day or night. Perhaps the most basic reason is the one given by the Internet's Mr. Showbiz, who wrote that Oprah is the "empathetic best girl-friend to the Betty Crocker set." It may be that more viewers prefer the lighter fare of daytime talk over the subject matter of evening talk shows, which are more news-oriented or erudite in contrast to what many critics call the sensational, sentimental, hokey, and true-confessional topics of daytime programs.

Television talk shows are as old as broadcasting, but their format is said to have been formed with the advent of Phil Donahue in the sixties. On occasion writers have compared daytime talk shows to soap opera because of the similarity of content, so it is not just happenstance that talk shows have replaced a number of soaps. However, scholars of popular culture also have linked the roots of the shows to nineteenth-century life, with its particular form of tattletale tabloids, theatrical melodramas, carnival acts, and advice columns for women in daily newspapers that became the fore-runners of "Dear Abby" and similar guides to living. Additionally, the pretelevision-era true-confession magazines, once the favored reading material in hairdressing salons, are considered precursors of talk shows. Covers from *True Story* and other confessional magazines predating World War II, framed and hung in restaurants such as the Cracker Barrel, are intended to capture a sense of a less-sophisticated era long since past. One such *True Story* cover, hanging in a Cracker Barrel restaurant on the north-south corridor of Interstate 95 obviously captivated its readers with the top headline: "Truth Is Stranger than Fiction." That and the title of the lead story, "My Own Love Trap" could easily be today's program on television. The links between such older forms of popular culture and today's talk shows reveal comparable selection of subjects considered appealing to women. Nothing is random in the choice of topics chosen by producers who not only are aware of women's interests but also watch rival programs, observe figures in the world of entertainment, and keep up-to-date with tabloid and gossip publications such as *The National Enquirer*, *Star*, *Globe*, and *People*. Until recently assertions that all talk shows, daytime or evening, had some of the same characteristics, are now only partly accurate. Since the nineties the focus of some day or evening programs has been altered, leading writers to note that even serious news programs have become more entertainment-oriented, while some daytime programs have offered more consequential discussions. Holding the interest and attention of a changing population is a never-ending major concern of networks. Perhaps the impetus to lighten evening talk came from the appearance on playful late-night comedy shows of such figures as President Clinton, Vice President Gore, and President Bush, all of whom took the opportunity to reveal themselves as so-called regular guys. Bill Clinton played his saxophone on network television; on "Saturday Night Live" Al Gore reprised the famous 2000 Democratic convention kiss. Following his nomination, Gore kissed his wife so ardently that it made the news shows. And, as for kissing, Oprah has been kissed by several presidential candidates, including George W. Bush, who also confided on the show that his favorite sandwich is peanut butter and jelly. Presidential wives Hillary Clinton and Laura Bush have appeared on Oprah's program as well.

On the opposite end of the spectrum, producers have attempted to increase the shrinking numbers of viewers of their regular evening talk programs by inviting reputable and prominent newsmen as guests. Members of every recent administration also have become frequent guests on night-time shows as well as Saturday and Sunday daytime talk shows. The popularity of the numerous weekend talk shows has networks vying for the same participants, who frequently go from one program to another. All sides gain mileage from such events: politicians presenting their views in what appears to be a less-partisan environment; and hosts in raising the bar on topics and issues.

Over a period of about 15 years, both weekend and numerous daily daytime talk shows, particularly the frivolous ones, were at their height, leading one journalist, Peter Carlson, to label them "America's great growth industry." Daily talk shows proliferated until the late nineties, when some of the more offensive programs were discontinued. But up to that time many became more and more sensational. No topic was taboo. The participants willingly shared personal and private elements of their lives with viewers, elements they hadn't told others. Even though doctors report that patients generally are reluctant to discuss sexual matters with them, it seems they are ready to go on television and tell all. Many of Oprah's shows support such discussions of personal matters.

Carlson, in preparation for an article examining the nature of talk shows, spent 24 hours in a motel, surfing television for such programs. In the article, he describes bits and pieces from a number of them: Phil Donahue, speaking on the advertising value of female breasts; Montel Williams, telling a man on his program to "put his butt in jail" until he stops hating others; Kathie Lee, humorously expressing her feelings about "too much gas"; Jerry Springer, emotionally advising a reformed Nazi about doing something else to gain notice, like taking off his clothing; Rush Limbaugh, mocking the homeless and their supporters; Jenny Jones, asking a 12-year-old guest why she has sex, and later ending her show with two requests for calls from people suspicious about their spouses' sex lives; Maury Povich, finishing up a show with clips of the next day's program— a woman who'd like to have sex with everyone in the city. Then, at four o'clock author Carlson clicked on "the legendary Oprah," whose topic for that day was the tragedies that befall television newspeople. When one guest spoke of being unable to go to the grave of his dead daughter, Oprah's response was "Wow," an expression she often uses when she appears to learn something for the first time.

When Oprah started in Chicago, in 1986, nobody anticipated the effect her program would have, particularly on Phil Donahue, then considered the irreplaceable monarch of daytime television. She was to usurp his position quickly, although she always credits him for his pioneering work on television, for creating "the one-topic format," that she emulated. She insists that his dissenting voice is important for the health of television. Because Donahue's show had established the pattern not only for Oprah but for all the other daytime talk shows that have since filled the air waves, for years a number of television reviewers praised the serious and creative Donahue programs. However, Donahue also has had multiple detractors, as has Oprah. One of Donahue's most severe critics was CNN evening talk show host, Howard Kurtz, who, finding little merit in Donahue's work, labeled him a man who seeks out causes—usually in questionable taste—in order to build audience following. In harsh language, Kurtz views him as "outrageous, self-righteous" and "moralistic." Yet, Kurtz concedes in passing that Donahue is more than a simple entertainer and refers to his having had presidential candidates on the show. Still, Kurtz focuses on the tawdry programs of Donahue and seems to find more shortcomings in him than in other television hosts. Kurtz and Donahue had a face-to-face television brouhaha in 1994 on a CNBC talk show hosted by Donahue.

But Kurtz doesn't give Oprah a pass either as he lists and describes numerous sensational topics explored on her show. He notes, though, as have other writers, that the time came when Oprah became uncomfortable with some of the occurrences on her program. Contending she had no desire to manipulate people or take advantage of their miseries, she said then and has repeated that her desire in life is to do good. Looking at her contributions to national and even international betterment, who can question her assertion? Kurtz, himself, in spite of his obvious cynicism and a certain mockery of the breadth of her statements, acknowledges the truths of her intentions. He credits her for changing from the model she followed when she first started.

From the beginning, talk shows have run the gamut from sleaze to serious. In that lineup Oprah's programs have almost invariably been ranked at the so-called classy end in both style and execution, leading to her top ratings at the annual Emmy Daytime Awards as well as a Lifetime Achievement Award. Substantive alterations took place in her telecasts once she decided to raise the level of her programs. During the years that competition increased among daytime talk shows and subject matter became more repugnant, *The Oprah Winfrey Show* made important strides toward abandoning the tawdry factor. While competitors seemed to compete for the title of most revolting and shocking, she enhanced the quality of her shows. Meanwhile, other hosts, among them Jerry Springer, presented such gross programs that one writer labeled them the "swamp." Needless to say, not all audiences appreciated Oprah's efforts to offer more quality programs. At times viewers have been fickle, preferring to tune in to Springer, not Oprah, so that popularity polls taken during the nineties reveal a seesawing between the two hosts. But even critics, who usually find daytime shows worthless, trashy, and objectionable, approved of the change, saying that Oprah's is the best show and a "blockbuster." That doesn't mean all journalists have credited her efforts to improve the caliber of talk shows; some writers whose field is television culture continue to fault her programs, overlooking those that have taken a 90-degree turn in the direction of memorable broadcasting. The anti-Oprah critics voice dismay at the role she plays in American cultural life, seeing her as pandering to and supporting mediocrity. She has been faulted as antimale. Black journalists, in particular, have expressed intense anger about what they see as her unfriendly attitude toward black men. Other critics consider her a purveyor of mishmash spiritualism and feel-good psychology; the term "touchy-feely" has been applied numerous times to her approach, and Oprah has been characterized as an untrained public confessor, who, along with most talk show hosts, has created in American life an unwholesome preoccupation with victimization. Both journalists and therapists have compared the self-help treatment preached on the shows as an emotional Band-Aid that undermines real therapeutic assistance. They stress the point that a talk show is just that, not therapy, and that all the people, including the guests, are simply performing.

Once Oprah decided to improve the nature of her program, she dropped many ignominious topics and added more professional guests, so that a number of the issues discussed have had serious and thoughtful analysis. On days when the country has been eager for solace as well as information about current events—the crash of the *Columbia* space shuttle, concerns about the probability that became the reality of the war in Iraq, worries about the economy, or careful consideration of other major happenings—*The Oprah Winfrey Show* attained stature commensurate with some of the best television offerings: the *NewsHour with Jim Lehrer* or memorable CNN broadcasts. On the eve of decisions involving Iraq, after a vital speech given by U.S. Secretary of State Colin Powell before United Nations representatives, both the regular February 6, 2003, Oprah broadcast on NBC and her Oxygen broadcast that followed focused on the problems confronting the nation and its allies in the consideration of war against Iraq. With the cooperation of individual writers, such as the well-known columnist on Middle Eastern affairs, Tom Friedman of the

New York Times, and several reporters from foreign countries, through the auspices of CNN, Oprah presented a lengthy program that allowed the airing of multiple points of view at home and abroad. This show was unusual because, unlike most of Oprah's other daytime offerings, it appeared to be completely unrehearsed and extemporaneous, even including an impassioned verbal assault on Tom Friedman's position by a member of the audience.

The program that followed, however—the Monday after that Friday airing of thoughtful, expert discussion—returned to a favorite, if not *the* favorite subject of all the programs: weight. If one could count the number of times a particular theme has been used on Oprah's show, weight would probably be the winner. Oprah has stated that the problem of weight is "huge." Viewers and writers alike speak of an earlier program on which Oprah pulled a cart of fat across the stage to demonstrate her own loss of body fat. She and her producers relish such memorable effects, either with her or the guests as performer. She periodically hosts programs about so-called emotional eating when her good friend Bob Greene is a guest. Because such shows stress the nature of self-help in controlling weight, much advice is given by both Greene and Oprah. He talks about the importance of exercise and organization, whereas she talks about writing thoughts in a journal so that the temptation to overeat becomes obvious. Greene and Oprah have a friendly, relaxed relationship; for example, when she confided that she had been snacking while doing her taxes, he tweaked her about the seriousness of her involvement in tax preparation, until she laughingly admitted that she was working with "the tax man."

Sometimes the comments by Oprah or visiting experts are used to emphasize the uninhibited nature of the show or guests. And, although there are far fewer sensational presentations than there were before she changed her focus, fewer does not mean zero.

Interspersed with prosaic or meaningful topics are some unusual confessions. For example, one recent subject was husbands who have sex changes. The program displayed the many characteristics of Oprah's presentations that account for her large numbers of viewers: so-called before and after photos of the guest; intimate revelations; emotion; humor.

Much ink has been spent on Oprah's style, which is always touted as refreshingly extemporaneous; that is, she doesn't like prepared scripts for herself, preferring a looser, more folksy approach. This same technique lost her a news announcer's job in Baltimore, yet led to her prodigious success as talk show host in Chicago. Although numerous articles speak of the spontaneity of the star, that is, her impulsiveness toward self-confession, various reporters have called this a scripted and managed action used to create a sense of authenticity. However, journalist Marcia Ann Gillespie defended her, saying that Oprah doesn't always speak pleasantries. Neither does she provide meaningless talk. Even when she appears to be asking and commenting instinctively, it results from careful advance preparation. On the opposite side, another critic disputes her authenticity, labeling her a con artist. Yet, still another, a well-known authority on male and female speech patterns, Deborah Tannen, has spoken of Oprah's natural ability at "rapport talk," which is typical of women's conversational patterns. In actuality, talk shows have very little spontaneity. Audiences have been led to believe that evening talk shows, such as *The Capital Gang,* are also a type of "shoot from the hip" production, but a profile of one of the panelists, Robert Novak, in the *Washingtonian* reports that Novak, having cultivated the persona of a curmudgeon, apparently different from his normal personality, deliberately takes provocative stands on issues in order to stir up opposition from his more liberal colleagues. Such behavior is attractive to the audience, and being seemingly unscripted allows Oprah to use her special type of humor that her audience delights in. On a show dealing with marital issues, Oprah injects humor that lightens the tension: "You have great sex; you're rolling around in bed, having a great time, and then the next morning you find he's still an idiot." The humor is not always so blatant; sometimes it is only suggestive, as was her response on the show about gender change; when her guest briefly described the genital surgery that had taken place, Oprah half hummed an old tune, "Yes, we have no bananas." Her guest—spontaneously?—changed the words to "yes, we have no vaginas." Unscripted? Perhaps, but probably not.

Her often risqué humor leads comedians to engage in some of their own with imitations. A memorable example occurred on *Saturday Night Live,* when the show satirized both Oprah and the title of a play with a portrayal of her interviewing first ladies in a session called "The Vagina Monologues."

On a program given over to fashion, in which the theme is a new look for fall, Oprah's humor punctuates everything: minidresses, denim, sweaters. Sometimes she'll speak mockingly of her own body, and as she looks at one of the sleek models, Oprah clowns; commenting on the wide separation between the breasts of the model, she asks with pseudo-innocence, "How do they do that?" But she does love clothes, as is evidenced in the hundreds of glamorous photos taken of her over the years. One year a full hour on the show featured the high-end designer Donna Karan, whose pricey clothing might not fit into the range of most Oprah watchers, but even if the audience doesn't buy the products, they enjoy the display. Then too, Donna Karan is known and honored for her charitable work, an important reason for Oprah's interest in having her as a guest. However, because she so enjoys shopping, Oprah often speaks about it.

On a related program the theme is "Looking Good," whose title belies the seriousness of the issue. Each guest once had to face the aftermath of a struggle between health and vanity. The first woman to tell her story is a television newsperson whose vanity was her hair, until she lost it to cancer. After wearing wigs to disguise her condition, she finally decided that her identity as a cancer survivor was more important than her hair, and from then on appeared on the show bald. A second guest relates her tale of having had one plastic surgery after another because she wanted to remain young and beautiful for her husband. The operations, however, left her with constant pain and severe nerve damage. Ironically, she lost everything—money, business, and her husband to another woman. A third guest who, in her attempt to look more glamorous, became a so-called sun worshiper, developed melanoma that destroyed parts of her face and teeth. And finally, a black woman, who was born an albino and suffered terribly during her youth, found herself through the acceptance of others when she went to college. On graduating, she became a teacher. This fourth and last segment of the show underlines the moral behind these stories about the destructiveness of vanity.

So much has been written about the effect of television on American culture and daily existence that many of the reviews, articles, and books begin to sound the same. Because television plays a central role as image maker in most of American life, scholars have examined every aspect of its impact on attitudes, behavior, philosophy, politics, and spending patterns on people here and around the globe. Most journalists agree that endorsements on television by high-profile celebrities of anything from merchandise to child rearing have more commercial worth than anything other individuals might provide. On all Oprah's programs, advertising, which occurs every few minutes, consumes huge amounts of time. During one show the advertisements shown were about cars, weight loss, animal food, bug spray, fast food, dishwashers, cheese, and syrup. Stars are part of the sales package of programs, issues, and merchandise. On the other hand, those programs (and magazines) also gain substantially through identification with various commodities. On a spring program, Oprah's modeling of an embroidered cotton tunic was what one reporter calls "the ultimate plug." Guided by the program theme, "Oprah's Favorite Things for Spring," Oprah "raved about" the tunic and the 18 other items exhibited. Boston Proper, the retail company selling the shirt, received a barrage of phone calls at the conclusion of the show, with the sales figures listed by the parent company, The Mark Group, as one shirt a minute. At another time, when Sylvester Stallone was the guest on a program, Oprah spoke of her preference for "T-shirt sheets" over the linens she'd had from Ireland and those from French villages where "little old ladies" had made them. In Chicago, the store Shabby Chic, which sold the item, had a run on jersey sheets the day after Oprah mentioned its name.

Companies are aware that women not only look at merchandise on television but purchase articles Oprah recommends. Oprah has a powerful effect on sales, as Paul Owers states in his article, "If Oprah wears it, watchers will buy." In the category of enhancement, after a particular bra was featured on Oprah's program, a Florida intimate apparel shop, knowing what a drawing card the Winfrey name is, ran a small ad to the effect that they carried the bra seen on Oprah's show. Small as the announcement was, it captured the attention of Palm Beach County women, many of whom bought the bra. Another time, after Oprah called attention to a medicinal compound that supposedly enhances a woman's sex drive, she brought on a flurry of phone calls to a small Maryland pharmacy making the custom mixture.

No matter the product, many affected companies have remarked on Oprah's extraordinary influence on sales. Because of the confidence she has instilled in audiences, they will follow her recommendations, says the president of one of the branches of Simon and Schuster, so that Oprah "creates markets all the time." On another show, half of the production provided a cooking demonstration by Art Smith, author of *Back to the Table* and Oprah's current chef. Smith's presentation gave Oprah the opportunity to clown and do a bit of sashaying around as she proclaimed her love of potatoes, always something she prefers over even desserts. The subject of food and the ways it is served provides the star the advertising opportunity to push the products of the chain "Crate and Barrel." As she gives prices, she softens the fact that she is advertising by humorously noting that she wants the discount being offered.

There is, however, a small group that questions the honesty of her recommendations. Finding almost everything Oprah does to be manipulative, commercial, and self-serving, one disgruntled former employee of Harpo published a lengthy screed about the star on the Internet. Claiming that Oprah has so-called business ties or a quid quo pro arrangement with large numbers of corporations, networks, and publishing houses, the writer calls her a "world-class phoney" who is able to deliver audiences because her name sells everything, and companies are not interested in how she does that. The author, Elizabeth Coady, who had been a senior associate producer for the *Oprah Winfrey Show*, wrote the piece as a form of protest against the confidentiality contract that restricts people for life for writing or talking about Oprah. Coady claims she wants to write a book about Oprah's operations—but the courts have upheld the agreements.

Although the millions of admirers far outnumber the critics, there are other dissenting voices besides Coady's. A book called *Everybody Loves Oprah* quotes and names some hostile journalists. One such journalist is P. J. Bednarski of the *Chicago Sun-Times*, who said in 1986 that Oprah was amoral about sexual matters and uninvolved with important moral and social issues. However, many of Oprah's activities, as well as the praise she has earned for them, seem to contradict Bednarski's statement in 1986 that Oprah was "unconcerned about social issues." The first thing most people say about the star is how much good she does. Other negative remarks quoted in the same book are by Bill Zehmer of *Spy* magazine, who voices dislike of her speech, her use of famous names, and her flippancy, and finds the people who work with her sycophantic. He even derides her appearance, as have many other journalists who seem in earlier years to have found that her Achilles' heel.

The frequency of exposure on television is also a major factor in selling a product or, as Stedman Graham labels everything, a "brand": books, movies, political positions, and even the politicians who espouse the positions. This fact explains the constant polling by companies employed to track the effect of so-called products that cannot be measured through sales figures. It is no surprise, then, that the benefits behind "sales" or image go in two directions, to the talk show and to the purveyor of a brand or product.

Almost every study of popular culture finds that television blurs the diversity of American life and culture. No matter the topic or guests, the underlying structure and values are those of middle-class America. Therefore, solutions to problems must conform to those particular values, which writer Barbara Ehrenreich describes as "the middle-class virtues of responsibility, reason and self-control." A type of lesson is delivered in the "guise of entertainment." Although not all talk shows nor their audiences are the same, Oprah's live audience generally is 80 percent white, middle-class, and female, and they want to hear about the problems of other women, even though the guests may very well come from a different social, cultural, or economic group than the viewers. Researchers inform us that viewers find it satisfying to hear people speak of their problems, whether or not they identify with the problem. There also is a type of catharsis in the very expression of what the audience regards as forbidden or sinful. In a sense it is similar to the appeal mystery and crime novels have for large numbers of readers. The most horrific plot and episodes are acceptable, even pleasing, to the least bloodthirsty individuals, because, as psychologists inform us, these individuals can have the experience without participation or any of the danger or consequences.

The harshest critics of the media find two opposing characteristics in daytime television: one is as amplifier and manipulator of the conventional, the ordinary, and the bland, which projects accepted stereotypes rather than exploring the wide differences in human behavior. Its opposite follows a different direction with a type of reductive tabloidization that sensationalizes, simplifies, and exploits individual narratives with a style that flattens everything into sound bites. Complex issues are watered down to suggest instant solutions and results. In the brevity of television time, drug or sexual abuse, poverty, violence, and other major social problems are shaped into manageable stories, the equivalent of three-act plays with introduction, development, and resolution. The most extreme conduct is turned into theater, and reality is replaced by that theater. In the course of an hour—minus the time out for numerous commercials—problems are presented, dramatized, discussed, and solutions appealing to audiences are found.

Daytime television is aimed at a mass audience, as are most movies, and it employs many of the same techniques that are based on the alterations of time. Inasmuch as the events narrated on the program took place previously, unlike real-life situations, they can be speeded up or slowed down; scenes are instantaneously cut from one to another; experiences and episodes, which in actuality may be unrelated, are collected and made to seem part of a "story"; most techniques of filmmaking are brought to bear through use of multiple cameras, zoom lenses, foregrounding or distancing of images, lighting and use of scenery, sound effects, and music. Background scenes from other sources clearly have been filmed in advance. To take a single example: on Oprah's program addressing the issue of cross-dressing and gender change, a guest's lifetime struggle, relationships with parents and siblings, wife, children, and the outside world, decisions and results were all explored within the limitations of a television hour.

Because of varying types of viewers, daytime and evening television have some important differences. Although both use celebrities and/or experts, the numbers are not the same, that is, daytime shows by and large, except for their hosts, are usually not dependent on such outside stars or pundits. Daytime programming seems to prefer everyday, average guests, whereas evening programs seek professionals. Most nighttime talk shows, with the exception of those hosted by comedians, focus on news or politics. Even though producers of both day and evening programs seek spirited participants who are not opposed to verbal conflict, the types of program participants are not alike.

Daytime shows "privilege ordinary people over experts" because their stories and exchanges are more personal and emotional, which is what audiences expect and tune in for. Hosts are seldom associated with a program's initiation, although the producer must always put the host in the forefront. The producer, who is usually female, must also find a new so-called take on stories to make them interesting. In fact, Ehrenreich claims "the plot is always the same." Thus, to capture the attention of the audience, producers constantly seek guests who are picked not only because of their stories but also for their personalities and looks; the producer seeks and deliberately fosters impassioned revelations from those they choose. Although the seeming simplicity of the presentation is actually artifice, as Jean Shattuc points out, very few viewers realize that the participant, that is, the nonexpert guest, has had what amounts to brief lessons in acting before the show; the producer and aides have coached the guests in what might be called "show and tell" methods. Like the director of a movie, the producer seeks to bring out the strongest kind of emotional presentation but also wants to keep it at a controlled pitch. Opposite to the so-called cool of professionals and experts, the nonprofessional guest with a narrative to tell is encouraged to reveal every feeling orally and physically, so that both the studio audience and the home viewer are caught up in the story. To avoid the occasional mistake, the producer thoroughly checks the backgrounds of guests in advance, from letters attesting to the truths of their stories to supporting statements, tapes, and pictures, and perhaps information from physicians. The producer must approve and even improve the participants' appearance, clothing, hair, and makeup prior to the program so that they are appealing to the audience.

Many people disagree about the significance of talk shows. The devoted followers who faithfully watch the programs claim that the shows add meaning and understanding to their lives. Almost without exception, viewers speak affectionately and admiringly of Oprah, frequently citing "the good" she has done. Some, who follow every story about her, talk as if a close relationship exists between them and the star. Former Harpo producer Coady describes reactions of audiences at shows: they "cry when

[Oprah] enters her television studio, gush when she speaks to them directly," and long to be touched. Journalists write of occasions when Oprah has left the stage to hug a member of the audience who has revealed a traumatic experience. All daytime hosts—unlike those on evening and weekend programs—present an aura of warmth, intimacy, and friendliness. Everyone is on a first-name basis, and most hosts, including Oprah, use personal pronouns as often as possible to create an informal atmosphere. Where some hosts hold a microphone while walking around, Oprah will sometimes sit in the audience, and, on occasion speak with a few people during the break. This may appear to be a spontaneous act, but in reality the producers have selected those people before the show. The conversation may then serve as a friendly transition between the segments of the show that have been broken by advertisements.

Some writers, popular culture scholars for the most part, find talk shows shameful, not necessarily because of the subject matter but because they believe the guests are exploited. Journalist Barbara Ehrenreich, describing the participants, sees them as so bereft of love, respect, and hope that they are willing, even eager, to reveal the most intimate aspects of their lives. Their homes, she claims, are "trailer parks and tenements." Many live in poverty; they may be on welfare or unable to pay their bills, or they may work two jobs to survive. No matter their situation, they are turned into exhibits for the purpose of entertainment. The guests often allow themselves to be humiliated, while the audience goes "slumming" says another writer. Some *New York Times* journalists have disparaged the shows; Janet Maslin called them "muck marathons," and Anna Quindlen described such programs as an airing of dirty laundry and the revelations as "the dark night of split levels."

Television, after all, is a business, and the entire venture is based on a syndicate's vision of viewers as a commodity that must be sold to advertisers who have a product to market. However, it falls to the producers to keep a show looking fresh and different from its competition. Generally with only a week to prepare each show, the producer is much like a newsperson working in a noisy office filled with every imaginable type of research file and publication. The subject matter, though, is social problems, not news, with emphasis on personal or domestic content. Although frequently shows move beyond the experiences or considerations of the "typical" viewer, the attraction is many-sided, with a fascination similar to that of human interest stories generally found in the "C" or "D" sections of newspapers, those favored by women. Yet, almost always underlying the content of the talk shows are views that are conservative, conformist, and moralistic. All of this is true of *The Oprah Winfrey Show*.

The audience at an Oprah show only appears to be selected at random. However, tickets are difficult to obtain and must be sent for long in advance, perhaps months before the program. They are not available at the door. Because certain colors do not photograph well on television, the studio audience is asked to avoid wearing beige or white and is expected to play an active role in the show, having usually been selected by a coordinator who wants the group to seem diverse. Writing for the *Sun Sentinel*, Kathryn Whitbourne recounted the details of her visit to the show. Security, on entry at the Harpo complex, included searches of handbags and removal of cameras, cell phones, and beepers, even taking away the writer's copy of *O*. While guests wait until their names are called for admission to the actual studio, they are free to visit a limited gift shop that sells almost no Oprah memorabilia. Surprisingly, considering Oprah's reputation for generosity, there are no giveaways for the general audience, only a box of tissues under the seat, for what Whitbourne ironically refers to as "those touching moments." Before the program some members of the audience, in addition to the guests, also have had coaching, and during the show the camera will focus on them. The lighting is directed toward those particular people, though the entire audience is expected to get involved, if only to applaud, ask questions, or show emotion. A warm-up precedes the program, and then the host appears.

Viewers who have watched talk shows for a period of time are aware of the structure followed by all of them, but one writer, Jean Shattuc, has formally broken that down into seven parts, describing a model, even to the number of minutes generally spent on each segment.

The first section is the longest, the last the shortest. Part one, introduction of the topic and guests by the host, consumes between 13 and 17 minutes, during which the host plays the perfect listener. The problem or challenge is explored, in part two, in 6 to 9 minutes, by various people— the host and members of the audience who ask questions and may contribute information about similar experiences. Part three is even shorter, 4 to 6 minutes, time partially expended by divergent points of view; at that point, if an expert is brought in, that person adds another tier of information to the matter. The audience is then given 3 to 6 minutes, in segment four, to question the expert. At that time other guests may be involved, or perhaps the host will abandon the role of listener and become a participant who tells her/his story. Once the issue has been developed and explored, the time has come to find resolutions, and 2 to 5 minutes are given over in part five to various possibilities; by then host and expert are on the same side, although the audience may not agree. Another 2 to 5 minutes, in part six, are spent in exploring possible answers and validation. The final segment, part seven, has almost no time to wrap things up, between 30 seconds and 2 minutes. The concluding statement, by expert, guest, or audience participant, is invariably hopeful and positive.

The show is usually taped several weeks in advance of its airing, providing the producers the opportunity to edit it, thus allowing some control over what is shown. The exceptions to the advance taping are those that cover breaking news and depend on immediacy for their impact on the viewers. Even though the audience is aware of most of the preparation and advance planning, few people resent it. Critics may question Oprah's sincerity and view her as a skilled actress, but viewers see her as natural; they approve, laugh, and applaud her outspokenness; so implicit is their trust in Oprah, they do not seem to know or care that everything on the program is managed.

With her five-day-a-week show, as well as specials, Oprah has worked with many celebrities over the years: movie stars, stage actors, singers, dancers, designers, writers, and worldwide celebrities. Some of the most famous include entertainers such as the insular Michael Jackson, in a 90-minute interview in February 1993, which was watched by a record number of 90 million people, and Madonna, another superstar who also attracted a very large audience. Among other celebrities whose appearance with Oprah caught the attention of television journalists was the Olympic champion figure skater, Oksana Baiul, because of her disagreement with Oprah about drinking—Oprah's candor contrasted with Baiul's defense of drinking as a Russian custom. Oprah's plain speaking, though, has its limits, as it did a few months later when Oprah refused to have Dennis Rodman on the show because she decided his newly published book was too risqué for her program.

Not everyone featured on the show is a celebrity, however. Some show participants are people from the everyday world of work. One program focused on individuals who worked for their employers for a long time, such as bellmen who worked for decades, never missing a day. Another time Oprah played a version of the *Dating Game* by inviting to her show in Chicago a single woman from east Columbia to meet with an unmarried television anchorman from Cleveland. Another type of show featured a young man who once had been caught up in the life of the street but rose to become a community leader. On the program he talked about a cherished subject of Oprah's—ways to solve basic problems of the country. Some years later, when one of those problems, violence, was the topic on the show, Oprah's guest was a nine-year-old boy who had formed an antiviolence group.

Violence, both personal and private and as a social issue, has long been an important subject for Oprah in many phases of her career—films, plays, articles in her magazine, and on her television programs. In 1992, in recognition of Martin Luther King, Jr.'s birthday, Oprah announced that she would undertake the topic "Racism in 1992" over the coming year in 13 different episodes. Shortly after she announced the forthcoming series, a black man named Rodney King was severely beaten by police after a traffic incident, and the trial that followed led to riots in Los Angeles. Oprah taped two programs examining the different sides of the event, with a mixed group of people discussing the jury's verdict and the riots that followed, as well as "the judicial system, and race relations." From January to November, the series covered many different topics related to violence: from racism and interracial hatred (including Japanese Americans and Native Americans) to fear and hate crimes.

Many writers—journalists and scholars alike—have emphasized the fact that Oprah is a highly visible black entertainer, yet her audience is predominantly white. Although on her program she frequently deals with racial matters and furthers activities of blacks in art and education, her race is apparently unimportant to her white viewers, yet central to her black viewers, while analysts regard her as "a comforting nonthreatening bridge between black and white cultures." Some of these perceptions result from her remoteness from both political activism and the civil rights movement. However, it has also been pointed out that the commercial aspect of her show, that is, the advertising, requires maintenance of a neutral stance on race.

Yet, in this particular series on violence, Oprah did not remain neutral. Although a variety of opinions were expressed, all the speakers agreed that racism is undesirable. Oprah's perspective on racism is described as "therapeutic," because she has said that the "lack of self-esteem" brought about "all the problems in the world." Numerous scholars fault that approach, which they name as "identity politics." Oprah insists that racists are ignorant and afraid. They must change their attitudes, and, unless they do, generation after generation will perpetuate the same biases. Language itself, even unknowingly, can be racist, and Oprah herself confesses to having used so-called racist expressions. Because anger solves nothing, she and the series facilitators said, it must be supplanted by forgiveness. People must change their attitudes, beginning in their hearts. Some scholars—among them Janice Peck—have criticized these views, however, as too subjective and too utopian for very complex issues.

One black member of Oprah's audience challenged the views expressed, telling her: "Listen Oprah, when you leave your show, you go to a lavish home. Lots of us don't go home to lavish things. We go home to empty refrigerators, you know, crying kids, no diapers, no jobs. Everybody ain't got it like everybody got it." Oprah has been faulted for failing to pursue the matter of inequality in politics and economics. According to the lengthy article by Janice Peck in *Cultural Critique*, when views of this sort were expressed on the show, the star would go to another speaker or a commercial. Thus, according to some analysts, the emphasis was on "individual transformation," which both Oprah and her "predominantly white, female constituency" favor over societal change.

Similar to the framing of the race series chiefly around the Rodney King episodes and their aftermath, a number of the Oprah Winfrey program subjects are topical matters that have been discussed in other media. The subject of DNA keeps surfacing as more and more lives are affected by revelations resulting from DNA testing. An entire Oprah show was devoted to some of the stories that have made news: some bizarre and painful and some satisfying in the search for justice and closure. On the bizarre side: a case involving the paternity of an eight-year-old child raised as their own by a husband and wife. After the death of the wife, a stranger came forward to claim the child as his because he'd had an affair with the wife. In another story, a sad but important result of DNA testing brought closure to the family of a young unidentified soldier who'd died years earlier in a plane crash in Vietnam, when DNA testing had not been developed. Circumstantial evidence led to the exhumation of his body, and a sample of the blood of the soldier's mother revealed a match. In yet another instance of the value of DNA testing, justice finally came in the case of a rape victim who had waited for six and a half years for evidence to pinpoint her attacker.

Health issues provide impetus for many programs, particularly when Oprah has experienced some of them. The entire world learns about the star's physical ailments when she shares personal information with them. Her rejection and then her acceptance of the idea of menopause gave rise to a publicizing of what one writer calls "the new attention-grabbing younger sister of menopause," called perimenopause. Many doctors approved the publicity given the problem, although other physicians and scientists objected to the commercial exploitation of the subject by various kinds of companies, with medicines, books, and supplements. Nevertheless, when the hour devoted to perimenopause on Oprah's program came to an end, the e-mail response was so overwhelming that it caused Oprah's Web site to crash.

A totally different type of health problem was the subject of a show that took place in 2002 following the case of a young mother, Andrea Yates, who murdered her children. This and similar tragedies became frequent subjects on television, with discussions and examinations of causes, treatments, and the families in which the tragedies took place. An Oprah program called "Post-Partum Depression" explored this grim subject, following the structure of most Oprah Winfrey programs, with several different stories, taped segments, testimony by some of those affected, an expert advisor—a doctor in this instance—and research data. The program provided much information and was different from the carnival setting and atmosphere that has surrounded other media presentations of the subject. Some talk shows often turn painful or tragic events into entertainment. On Oprah's show, an expert provided definitions and explanations of differences between postpartum psychosis and depression. Because approximately 200 children each year become the victims of emotionally ill mothers, the doctor and others on the program warned the studio audience and home viewers of the many fallacies surrounding such illnesses and described the actions that need to be taken inside and outside the family, treatments, successes, and failures.

In spite of the important educational value of the program, talk shows often use sentimental techniques to arouse the audience to great emotional heights. In this show, tender photos of the murdered children and videotape of candlelight vigils following their deaths elicited feelings of bathos. Excess sometimes takes over to the detriment of the somber warnings; one such example followed the story of a mother who drowned her baby son, with pictures of the murdered child's father weeping at the infant's grave.

Emotion on the show is not always focused on the sorrowful. One Valentine's Day show focused on happiness. The subject was the love of spouses for mates who had sacrificed much for them, and the handful of people chosen for the show were rewarded during the program. In one instance a wife whose husband had been too poor to give her an engagement ring and had defied his family's choice of a bride for him was given a two-carat diamond ring; a man, who had given up all the money he'd saved for a Harley Davidson of his dreams when he married a single mother of five children, was given a $20,000 Harley bike; and a couple in their eighties, married more than 60 years earlier during World War II in a simple wedding on an Army base because the girl's father had died, were given a surprise second wedding. The camera scans the audience, all of whom appear to be crying. Oprah pronounces the ring "beea-u-ti-ful." Of course, every show has an advertising component, and Oprah mentions the names of the gift-giving companies several times throughout the program.

The variety of subjects and guests obviously account for part of the popularity of the *Oprah Winfrey Show*. Only on rare occasion are one day's subjects related to the next. The exceptions are national or world events of such magnitude that the entire country is caught up in them. One subject that engrossed all of the United States and much of the world for a long period of time was the terrorist attacks on the World Trade Center Towers in New York and on the Pentagon in Washington, D.C., on September 11, 2001. Following those incidents Oprah had a series of different kinds of programs about the effects and aftermath of the events. On other occasions, she had also participated in patriotic activities unrelated to her show.

Several of the programs were designed to include her audience—which had clearly been picked beforehand. With Oprah serving as moderator, on September 17 and 25 the audience interacted with the experts; on the first date the guests were Senator Joseph Biden, of the Senate Foreign Relations Committee, and Judith Miller, a writer for the *New York Times*, whose special area of knowledge is the Middle East and Osama bin Laden. With scenes of the tragedy, groups of people at ground zero, pictures of the flag and the Statue of Liberty, and prayerful songs, the emotional level of the show was extraordinary. On September 25, the interaction was between the audience and the psychologist, Dr. Phil McGraw, at that time a regular Tuesday guest on Oprah's show. In his usual role of advisor, Dr. McGraw discussed the anger, fear, and frustration that resulted from the personal and national catastrophe. His counsel was to focus on the importance of dealing with fear and to put off life-changing decisions when one is in a state of turmoil.

The following Tuesday, Dr. McGraw's interaction was with individuals who had suffered personal losses in the destruction of the towers. His analysis and discussions, though, were applicable to tragedy of many kinds. Listing the four stages of grief—shock, denial, anger, and resolution, he spoke of "grief work" and the need for life strategies for the bereaved when others move on with their own lives. He recommended concentrating on day-to-day things, not life goals, and contrary to the old adage about time as a healer, he said emphatically that time heals nothing. One has no option but to get past the pain. However, he admonished, the survivor must be willing to ask for and accept help and set up a support system. Dr. McGraw's advice to all the bereaved was sensible and practical. On the other hand, Oprah imparted a spiritual message, saying the loss of a loved one is the "gain of an angel"; yet, when Oprah began to speak of angels, the pragmatic psychologist quickly shifted the discussion back to the realistic view. Reality, however, includes the showing of commercials, which though jarring, were a symbolic "getting on with life."

One of Oprah's more memorable tributes to the tragedy came on her program "Music to Heal Our Hearts." Oprah's shows are frequently emotionally charged and this one was more so than most, and on this one she seemed to run the gamut from humor and laughter to singing and weeping. Revealing her love of gospel music and its healing power, Oprah noted that she played gospel music while she was on her treadmill. She was obviously moved when a white performer, Sam Harris, following the style of black gospel singers, rendered "Precious Lord" and "You'll Never Walk Alone." Briefly breaking the somber mood, she joked about an occurrence at the memorial service at the National Cathedral when she'd been asked the name of the black singer at the event (Denyce Graves): she told the audience something she has said on other occasions—that white people seem to think all blacks know each other. At another point, the religiously educated Oprah showed her knowledge of biblical passages after two entertainers sang "Bridge over Troubled Waters."

Perhaps the highlight of the program came with the introduction of the earlier-mentioned superstar for whom Oprah's admiration seemed unbounded. The opera diva Denyce Graves skipped a performance of the Washington Opera in order to be on Oprah's show, after Oprah invited her following her National Cathedral performance the previous week. At the end of Graves's aria, Oprah told the audience to stand, and the next song was "Stand," a gospel favorite of Oprah's.

Toward the end of the program, following talk of prayer and healing, Oprah, who had left the stage to sit in the audience, joined in the singing and swaying of the emotionally-charged audience. As one last song was sung, with a dedication "to the firefighters and all those who put themselves in harm's way," Oprah was shown in her seat in the audience, singing while a backdrop of the New York firefighters appeared. Among her many, many emotional shows, this one surely stands out.

Oprah has periodically taken to the road with a "Live Your Best Life" tour. She began her biennial project in 2001, a "personal crusade" that she says she plans to continue even after she turns 50, so that all her followers will look forward to becoming 50.

In the summer of 2003, accompanied by two of her dogs (with a dog handler), she came to the Convention Center in Philadelphia, the fourth and last city of her summer tour, where she addressed her mostly female audience of 2,700. Calling her "the Amazon queen of touchy-feely," David Hiltbrand, a reporter for the *Philadelphia Inquirer*, describes the crowd as "screaming" upon her arrival in a limousine and "practically levitating" when she took the stage. Although the cost of tickets was high—$185 per person, and sometimes much higher when purchased elsewhere, most of the crowd seemed to think it was worth it. What they did get, writes Hiltbrand, "was a cross between a revival meeting and a self-help [one day] seminar." Oprah often refers to her work as a mission, and, according to the statistics of *Fortune* magazine, these four-city self-affirmation tours, which inspirit the thousands of women ticket holders, bring in more than a million and a half dollars.

Typically, the rules for the event were similar to those of her television show; attendees didn't know the subject matter in advance or the format; they were not allowed to have a photo taken with the star; nor were they permitted to seize the microphone during the afternoon session, when members of the audience participated.

During the two-hour morning program, Oprah spoke about her own life from her grandmother's farm in Mississippi to her African trip during the Christmas season in 2002. The message of her talk was of the need to find "the seed of grace" in the unhappy episodes of existence. Her own bad experiences—"she recounted plenty of these," writes Hiltbrand—involved "diets, hair and shoes." The two-hour, afternoon, so-called sharing session with speakers selected by Oprah focused on the same types of problems aired on her television shows, related to marriage, sickness, and weight. Among the large numbers of mothers and daughters in the audience, many seemed to be enthralled, some describing themselves as edified and inspired by the star's message that they "rise above circumstances and expectations to pursue their souls' distinct destinies."

Through television over the years, Oprah helped advance a number of careers, the most successful of which is that of psychologist Phillip Mc-Graw. So striking were his regular appearances on the *Oprah Winfrey Show* that after several years, with the support of Oprah's Harpo, Paramount, and King World Productions, he launched his own program on September 16, 2002. Known by the folksy name "Dr. Phil," he reportedly received the highest talk show ratings of anyone since Oprah hosted her first Chicago program. He has been compared to the former television gurus, Dr. Joyce Brothers and Dr. Ruth Westheimer, but columnists have noted that he is tougher and more audacious.

Before he met Oprah, McGraw was a resident of Wichita Falls, Texas, and a courtroom strategist with his litigating consulting firm Courtroom

Sciences, Inc. Members of Oprah's staff have talked of her role in his success on television, saying, "without her, he'd still be a no-name shrink in Texas." Long before forming what became a multimillion-dollar consulting firm with a close friend in Dallas, he had several different careers. After getting his doctorate from Midwestern State University, he followed the path of his father, who had come to his own career as a psychologist in his forties. Each of them traveled from one small town to another in their practice as therapists, but after a time their relationship soured and they ended their practice. When the son lost interest in the traditional field of therapy, he moved into consulting. Then, in 1996, he met Oprah when she was in Texas defending herself in the so-called Mad Cow case brought by the beef companies. Her lawyers brought McGraw in to assist them, and in the process he became a friend and advisor to the star. Oprah credits him with helping her to win.

Two years later he joined the *Oprah Winfrey Show* on a once-a-week basis as an expert on life strategies and relationships and soon was considered by a number of television fans as *the* expert on relationships. Oprah called him "A walking, talking, in-your-face reality check."

Like others who have worked with or for Oprah and appeared on her show, McGraw became a best-selling author. In his 1999 book *Life Strategies*, his first acknowledgment is a thank-you to Oprah for awakening and inspiring him. As did chefs and exercise trainers who wrote best-selling books after she introduced them on her television show, he claims his book wouldn't have come into being without her. He expresses gratitude for her friendship and for allowing him to share her program. With the highest of accolades, he describes Oprah much as Jesse Jackson had some years earlier: as "the brightest light and the clearest voice in America today." In the introduction he talks about the court case and calls her the most consequential woman in the entire planet, and in the first chapter he invokes her name constantly. He promises the female reader that she too can be like Oprah by learning and following "the rules of the game" in dealing with the affairs of life.

On Oprah's show the terms most frequently associated with Dr. Phil were "Get Real" and "Tell It Like It Is," and probably his best-known appearances carried the label "The Get Real Challenge." Beginning with what Oprah labeled the "season premier" on September 10, 2001, Oprah and Dr. McGraw described a number of sessions that would be seen weekly and talked about what was to come. A group of 42 participants were chosen from 15,000 applicants—black, white, Asian, male and female, ages 23–63—who had responded to a request for the psychological series with letters about their problems and wishes. Of the 42 selected, seven were singled out specifically for the taping of their stories for the show. The other 35 remained part of the background in a role somewhat reminiscent of an ancient Greek chorus. Every Tuesday the group would be seen on television as their various problems were aired.

The background material was alternately described and taped so that the viewers could follow along more easily. In the tapes and explanation the participants met, unhappily had to pick roommates, and were said to be anxious. The following day they were made up by an expert crew and bused to the studio, where they were introduced to Dr. McGraw for the first time. They were together for five days of sessions. McGraw didn't allow questions, and he was shown to be rude and on the attack. When Oprah called him "mean" she was identifying with the reactions of the audience and viewers, but he explained that niceness is a waste of time. He laid down the law, said Oprah, and then, in the taped material he described the rules and guidelines: there could be no gossip, no sexual interaction, no changes in major activities for the next 15 days. These restrictions were created to help the participants avoid impulsive decisions. No watches were to be worn, and people had to complete the training of the five-day schedule. The large group was divided into small ones, each with a member leader of the team. Everyone had to answer questions about what was going on in his/her life, and what was not. Reminding the participants of the seriousness of the undertaking, Dr. McGraw asserted that the program was not about entertainment but about changing lives.

The situations of the seven people who were the focus of the series ran the gamut from different types of molestation, to bullying, to issues of bulimia, to divorce and abandonment, to rape, and extreme anger. In strong, blunt language, when McGraw deemed it necessary, he told male and female guests alike to pick up their "butt," and do what was necessary to change their predicaments and lives. Sometimes he yelled, and in one instance called a participant "a whiner" who "needs to wake up and be a man." Yet McGraw's advice had a common thread in all these varied cases: nothing can be done about the past; forgive yourself and move on with your life. Sometimes he or the group hugged the neediest guest. Then, through the magic of television, the finale of the program featured a so-called fast-forward to the events that followed the end of the series over a period of time. Each of the seven featured participants had taken action, from divorce, to weight loss, to talking and reconnecting with people, and going to college or graduate school.

As a happy, goodbye gesture, the group put on a little show that included reading limericks and having some fun with their mentor, Dr. Phil. He thanked everyone tearfully and warmly, telling them how honored he felt to have been in their lives. His final words reminded them that we are all seen as fixed in certain roles and other people don't want us to change. But we must all walk out of our history and move on.

Following the typical formulaic structure, Oprah had the last word; she congratulated McGraw; and some final photos were shown of the guests, who also spoke briefly about the experience and what it meant to them.

Oprah and Dr. Phil have proven to be very different. On her programs and later on his own, he was able to be more folksy and outspoken than she and discuss subjects that Oprah had in a sense eschewed, the most intimate issues about sex. Nevertheless, even in the years since she began to avoid controversial personal matters, some journalists and a few viewers have objected to her programs on incest, sexual abuse, homosexuality, and recovered memory about sex. Oprah has said that she plays a very important role for her audience, with open and frank discussions, as well as comments and advice about the so-called untouchable subjects. In several interviews she professed that her program offers something of a spiritual and religious component because as a knowledgeable and positive-thinking host, she has said that she offers the equivalent of a ministry. This idea could be compared to a reviewer's comment about a recent Joan Didion book, in which one of his remarks also seems applicable to Oprah: "The roles of candid observer and polemicist at times coexist uneasily."

Where critics might fault Oprah as they have other talk show hosts for treating topics that are voyeuristic, popular culture scholars have noted that such programs become acceptable under particular circumstances, that is, the inclusion of experts. Because Dr. McGraw is a psychologist and therefore an expert, he provides an entirely different view of many Oprah Winfrey programs for the critics.

Still, like Oprah, Dr. Phil McGraw cannot escape being the focus of occasional humor. Oprah's "never, never" was her response to lighthearted bumper stickers in Seattle during her 2003 "Live Your Best Life" tour. The words proclaimed, "Oprah for president," leading one columnist to suggest that followers put her name on a write-in ballot and add "Dr. Phil to complete the ticket."

Chapter 4

BOOKS AND MORE BOOKS

Always looking for ways to maintain the attention and involvement of her audience, and with an eye on ratings, Oprah and company introduced what was at that time a novel idea, a monthly television book club. Its popularity led other shows and television channels to adopt the idea. Oprah chose a book she had read and enjoyed and then announced the name on the air; a program featuring an appearance by the author of the book followed; and finally a group of diverse, carefully picked, packaged, and screened readers discussed the book on the air. Oprah chose a book every month, except in summer, although no regular day was scheduled for the club to be on the program. Before the choices were announced on the air, sealed boxes of books were sent to public libraries with the labels "Do Not Open Until–." With the usual declarations, hype, and advertising, the club began in 1996; the first book discussed was Jacqueline Mitchard's *The Deep End of the Ocean*.

From the beginning to its demise in April 2002, everything chosen by Oprah became a best seller and an exceptional boon to the publishing industry. For both writers and publishers, it was the equivalent of hitting the lottery. Throughout the country, bookstores, large and small, knowing the effect of Oprah's pronouncements, immediately stocked numerous copies of the recommended book. Even a writer's first novel could sell as many as a million copies. *Publishers Weekly*, backing up the data about Oprah's influence, claimed that hardcover and paperback books could not get onto best-seller lists unless readers knew the author's previous work or were an Oprah pick.

Once Oprah's Book Club became a reality, many bookstores and coffee shops had special displays of books advertised as "An Oprah Selection." Her chosen books even had an imprint to that effect. Only a year after the introduction of the book club, *Newsweek*, along with others, labeled Oprah as the most significant person in the modern book world. One *Newsweek* writer, in reviewing a thriller, had words of advice for publishers about turning their books into best sellers, and that was to "pray for an act of God, Imus, or Oprah." Inspirational books, even if not part of Oprah's club, became very popular as a result of exposure on her show, particularly after the events of 9/11. One was a book of poetry, *Heartsongs*, whose success was fueled by a visit of the 11-year-old author who suffered from a severe form of muscular dystrophy. Not only did his first book become a best seller, but after his appearance on Oprah's show, the child signed a five-book contract. Oprah called him inspirational and her "friend," as well as "an angel on earth." In a lengthy report of the story, journalist Robert Elder comments: "Sentimental? Yes. But publishers have found that sentimentality sells." Elder, publishers, and Oprah are not the only people involved with books who have discovered the value of sentimentality.

Washington Post staff writer David Streitfeld compared Oprah's effectiveness in getting people interested in books to that of nineteenth-century tycoon and philanthropist Andrew Carnegie who, among his other deeds, endowed 2,500 libraries. But a colleague of Streitfeld's on the same paper was not as fulsome with her praise, raising the possibility that Oprah simply harvested the returns of a recent national revival of reading. Nonetheless, so influential was Oprah considered in her effect on national reading habits that in 1999 the National Book Foundation, at an elegant black-tie affair hosted by actor and comedian Steve Martin, presented her with its fiftieth-anniversary gold medal.

Accepting the medal, Oprah spoke of the paramount role books had played in her life. Books, she said, have always been the most pleasurable part of her existence. They helped her to learn about herself and the world. Singling out Maya Angelou's autobiographical work *I Know Why the Caged Bird Sings*, she called it a work of validation for her when she was a poor, black, southern-born teenager who had suffered many hurts. For the first time, she understood that it was possible to move beyond her misery to a better life. At that point, she said that she began to understand the force of writers and their books.

Yet, in spite of her passion for books, and after several years of praise for her effect on the publishing industry and the reading public's increased interest in books, Oprah, nicknamed the "queen bee of book clubs," suddenly decided to abandon the club as part of her television show. On a Friday show, she informed the audience that the novel *Sula* would be the last book chosen for the club. She announced, rather thoughtlessly, in a statement that immediately provoked criticism, that she no longer could find interesting books to read, introduce, and discuss on her program. Although Oprah did not tell the audience of other factors in her decision, there was more to the matter than lack of worthy books.

Regardless of the huge number of books sold, from 600,000 to 1,000,000 new copies per book, a market survey revealed only a limited viewing audience for the television discussion of books, considerably less than those who watch the regular day-to-day programs. Soon the shows about books became less frequent: when first started, there was a new book nearly every month; in 2000, there were nine; and in 2001, there were six. Although various types of experiments with the format were tried to maintain interest—informal dinners and conversations with authors, filmings of dramatic scenes from books, even discussions with women whose life experiences were like those of the book characters—the numbers of viewers dropped. Also, sales of books were said to be flattening out. However, a typical "inside source" claimed that the task of screening a book a month was exhausting for Oprah and her staff, "the single hardest thing" that had to be done for the television program.

Some of the publishing companies supported Oprah's decision publicly—after all, how could they do otherwise, given the important financial boost she'd made to the industry. Random House put a full page "Thank you, Oprah" ad in the April 12, 2002, edition of the *New York Times*. The company expressed gratitude for the years of work she'd devoted to "books, authors, and readers." Nevertheless, it was a serious and unexpected blow, and several spokesmen felt her statement that she could find no interesting books to read was an unjust disparagement of American publishing. The demise of the club unquestionably was a great disappointment to many writers who had hoped to be chosen, but it meant much more to the publishers who had made many millions from the sales.

Reviewers also were skeptical about the reason given. As Carlin Romano of the *Philadelphia Inquirer* rightly pointed out, the final book Oprah picked, *Sula*, had been written 28 years earlier by Toni Morrison, one of four Morrison novels Oprah had chosen during the lifetime of the book club. Given that lengthy time stretch of which Oprah had availed herself, Romano questions why "out of decades of published fiction in English" she was unable to recommend a single novel each month for the club. Ro-

mano's piece turns even more derisive with the ironic comment that anyone as rich as Oprah would certainly give up the arduous task of a monthly
book selection and take an easier road for her program "like talking between commercials or serving in the Israeli Defense Forces."

In June, shortly after Oprah's show discarded the book club, Katie
Couric and Matt Lauer's *Today* show adopted the idea of a somewhat different literary endeavor. Undoubtedly influenced by the demise of
Oprah's club, it bore some resemblance to her book club. Women were
the primary audience, inasmuch as both Oprah's and the *Today* show are
presented at times considered more accessible for women than men and,
on both, the program material focused on women. The format for the
Today club was different in that a well-known author rather than the
show's host announced his/her choice of a current work by a lesser-known
author. The announcement of the fascinating and "don't miss" book was
followed up a month later with a discussion by a group of people who are
members of an existing club.

Even though she ended the book club, some people still associate
Oprah with books, though at times, critics have made some negative
statements about her choices. A mixed message appeared in a generally
favorable review of Patricia Henley's novel *In the River Sweet,* in which
Carol Doup Muller faulted the "piling on of 'Oprah' topics that swamp" it.
Although she listed the topics without comment, they were reminiscent
of the themes of Oprah's programs—and of articles in her magazine as
well—lesbianism, abuse, osteoporosis, devotion, retardation, and "a crisis
of faith." Other critics included deprecatory comments about Oprah's subject matter in reviews of novels, faulting many of her choices as focusing
on dysfunctional people. Some reviewers found Oprah's selections exces-
sively similar. For instance, a *Wall Street Journal* writer, Cynthia Crossen,
said that the reach of Oprah's book selections went from "A (abused) to B
(battered)." One reviewer seemed enigmatic at best in an evaluation of
Oprah's preferences, when he suggested that the term "woman's novel"
should be dropped, and "the Oprah novel" should be substituted because
all her selections had the same formula.

The lame excuse given for *The Oprah Winfrey Show's* abandonment of
the book club had numerous people wondering about Oprah's judgment.
Newspapers played it up in ways that had to make her uncomfortable.
There was a loud, sometimes angry outcry, and not a little scorn from readers, comedians, and even comic strip artists. There were also humorous
comments, as well: a little-known columnist headlined one of his reports as
"Oprah's Shelved, So Others Must Pass on the Good Word." With strong,

tongue-in-cheek language, Ben Crandell, who writes about the famed South Beach, Florida, scene, called Oprah's dismissal of the club "Betrayal. Intrigue. Ruthlessness.... heartless...shocking...callous...."

Another farcical illustration of the mileage gained from the clumsiness of Oprah's action appeared in a mocking comic strip, drawn by cartoonist Matt Janz. Titled "Out of the Gene Pool," the strip shows two figures, one black, one white, looking at television and listening to Oprah speaking of the ennui she had felt in reading while she ate her lunch; no longer interested in the book because of boredom, she put a carrot in her nose, she tells her viewers, and the experience, which she describes as "spiritual," provides "rebirth." Making fun not only of Oprah's sudden loss of interest in books but also of her media personality, the cartoonist satirized both the star and the audience. An easy target for ridicule in her pronouncement about the disappearance of worthwhile books and her public personalizing of all her experiences, she became a satirist's dream. Mockingly, Janz played up her media personality, her interest in things spiritual, and her unsuspected but apparent belief in the phoenix myth—regeneration from ashes. Oprah, in this strip, characteristically reveals everything to her audience because she wants to include them in her awakening, the great phenomenon of renewal. But what an awakening she has had, she tells the audience, the abandonment of books for carrots. While playing on Oprah's relatively newfound interest in good food and health, the cartoonist surely was looking back humorously at a centuries-old debate about mind and body. However, he skillfully conflated the body, that is the carrot, with spirit. In other words, Oprah's renewal comes from a vegetable, not from some clever or brilliant thesis or work of art.

The two characters shown in the strip are next seen reacting with some astonishment to the huge headline and lengthy stories that appear in the next day's newspapers. Outranking the size of headlines and scope of other news reports are the accounts of the latest activity of many thousands of women who are followers of Oprah; in order to get carrots to thrust up their noses—and experience what Oprah did, they overrun grocery stores and hospitals and bring about a surge in the stock market. All of this, as imagined by the cartoonist, is of greater import than the news of the capture of Osama bin Laden or the announcement that a cure had been found for cancer.

Only six years after she introduced the first of her series of books, Oprah's Book Club was put to rest in the summer of 2002. Was it predictable? Did the majority of readers like her choice of books? Apparently so, considering the vast number of sales. Oprah's good friend, writer Maya

Angelou, had weighed in, stating she didn't agree with all the choices, but that reading is what mattered. If, indeed, lack of audience interest was the problem—rather than the so-called limit of good, readable books—could the cancellation of that feature in the show have been premature? Considering the vast amount of publicity given to the dustup Oprah and company had with one of her chosen novelists, Jonathan Franzen, shortly before the decision to give up the book segment of her program, the interest of readers and nonreaders, as well as general interest throughout the country, in the book selections was aroused to a pitch not enjoyed before, and could only have served to swell the numbers of the show's audience.

Franzen's third novel, *The Corrections*, became a best seller from the moment it was announced as an upcoming selection of Oprah's Book Club. The blurb that appeared on the jacket of his next book, *How to Be Alone*, a collection of essays, described *The Corrections* as "the best-loved and most-written-about novel of 2001." The effect of Oprah's choice of Franzen's novel was much like that of other books chosen for that distinction, and, like them, the question arises whether, no matter how deserving, it would have entered the world of best-sellerdom without that association. *Washington Post* book reviewer Jonathan Yardley thinks not.

Calling Franzen a writer from "the high-art literary tradition," Yardley pointed out in his discussion of *The Corrections* that he, unlike "some" critics, didn't much care for Franzen's two previous novels because they were "preachy" and "sermonizing," and what is more, he noted, they were not very successful commercially. Yardley concluded that an Oprah choice for the book club was an absolute guarantee of financial success, and, in his annoyance with Franzen, Yardley suggested that the novelist's third work of fiction would not have done much better than Franzen's previous ones without Oprah's imprimatur. He made no concessions to Franzen's talent, unlike some other reviewers. One admiring reviewer, Richard Locayo, writing a year later, asserted that Franzen's mind was "one of the most nuanced...in the dwindling world of letters." Yardley, however, did not want to be seen as a fan of *The Oprah Winfrey Show* and wrote a second piece called "The Story of O, Continued." While repeating his belief that Oprah genuinely championed books, he also informed his readers that he thoroughly disliked her television program. The one time he watched it, he says, he "nearly gagged on all the treacle and psychobabble."

Other book critics noted that 46 successive books anointed by Oprah have become best sellers since September 1996. *New York Times* reviewer David Kirkpatrick said that Oprah's choice of Franzen's book may have brought in as much as a million and a half dollars to the author, and he quoted Lewis Lapham, editor of *Harper's,* as saying "A good writer is a rich writer, and a rich writer is a good writer." Although many less than rich writers might quarrel with Lapham's statement, there is no question that many of those chosen by Oprah have joined the millionaire ranks. Commenting on Franzen's reference to the "high-art" literary tradition, Yale professor, critic, and defender of that faith, Harold Bloom, weighed into the argument, claiming he'd be honored to have Oprah select him, an event not likely to occur, given the subject matter and density of Bloom's work.

Franzen, in the eyes of some, or many, undoubtedly had committed the unpardonable sin of ingratitude for becoming one of the chosen. In a humorous aside about Oprah's club, reviewer Carlin Romano stated that Franzen's response to Oprah's picking his novel was "as if he'd been tapped by the Springer Book Club," whereas *U.S. News* labeled Franzen "the unchosen one." Franzen had announced that he didn't like the placement of Oprah's Book Club logo on the cover of his novel, because, he said that he rejected the idea of "corporate ownership." Objecting to being placed in a class that included "schmaltzy one-dimensional" books, he said—saying different things to different readers—that he classifies his book as belonging to the high-art tradition. And although he found popular writers like Scott Turow and Stephen King "honorable," he was convinced that they were on the covers of *Time* magazine due to the large amount of money promised in their publishing contracts rather than their importance to American culture. Franzen derided the effect of money on American culture and stressed that money is the catalyst behind photographs on the covers of *Time.* Franzen expressed a belief in "social instruction" as the most important element of fiction and mourned some of the changes that have come about with the twentieth-century novel.

Although Franzen somewhat grudgingly asserted that Oprah was "smart and...fighting the good fight," that is, getting people to read, clearly and after the fact, ironically, he did not want to be known as one of Oprah's Book Club choices. He identified with the philosophy of novelist William Gaddis about the need of serious writers, even at the price of being "obscure," to resist the "culture of inauthentic mass-marketed" images because of the dangers of becoming those very images. Franzen's own issues with the marketplace were part of a philosophy that led to his public and private pronouncements and his verbal rejection of television in general. The result of the brouhaha was Oprah's cancellation of an appearance by Franzen on her show, yet, according to some news reports, she did not retract her selection of the book. However, *Newsweek* reviewer Jeff Giles, with a punning title to his column "Errors and 'Corrections,' " said Oprah had conceded that Franzen wouldn't be on her show but appeared to suggest that her viewers might as well give up reading *The Corrections*.

In *How to Be Alone,* his essays published a year after *The Corrections,* Franzen stated that Oprah disinvited him from the book club because she considered him "conflicted," but the jacket cover on his book of essays finds his narrative about the experience to be "rueful."

More people agreed with Oprah than with Franzen. In addition to her loyal audience and readers, many journalists supported Oprah's side in the disagreement, calling Franzen stinging names that he duly records in his essay "Meet Me in St. Louis." To a writer in *New York* magazine, he was a "motherfucker"; to a writer in *Newsweek,* a "pompous prick"; an "ego-blinded snob" to a writer in the *Boston Globe*; and to a writer in the *Chicago Tribune,* a "spoiled, whiny little brat."

Prior to these events, when he was still an unannounced selectee on Oprah's list, Franzen was filmed in his home state of Missouri by a team consisting of a television producer, a photographer, and a crew from the Oprah show in preparation for the segment that would be done about his novel. A producer had told him there were some difficulties of approach to his novel and they wanted to try several things for the presentation. Not only would there be a summary of the work but also included would be some brief background about Franzen as well as a filmed part in which he would be speaking. Puzzled by the focus on his life in St. Louis, the author pointed out in his essay, "Meet Me in St. Louis," that he may be a Midwesterner, but he is one who had lived in New York for the past 24 years. With that statement, quoted directions from the producer and cameraman, and his own choice of words such as "pretend," he established his disapproval of the entire commercial process and his distaste for what he considered the hokeyness of television. Nevertheless, he decided during the shoot that he would be Midwestern if that was what's necessary for the program. However, Franzen and the crew failed to agree on any number of things in the process of filming. He and the producer of the spot filmed for later showing seemed rarely to be in agreement, with the single exception—that the entire piece they were putting together about him was "totally bogus."

In contrast to many writers, Franzen has an inordinate sense of privacy, something any reader of his pre-*Corrections* work would have immediately grasped, and in all fairness to Franzen, it should be pointed out that there have been other Oprah selectees who vetoed the publicity that went with selection. Ursula Hegi, for example, whose second novel followed her first as an Oprah choice, rejected a jacket blurb to that effect. A Simon and Schuster publicist defended the decision as an act of privacy.

Franzen could not—perhaps did not entirely want to—escape the controversy. He kept waffling back and forth. When *Today* host Katie Couric introduced him as someone who'd committed "an Oprah no-no" and humorously invited him to dish some dirt, Franzen took the entire blame for the episode. He expressed gratitude to Oprah, depicting her as dignified and gracious, whereas he had acted badly. His excuse for his bad behavior was that he'd forgotten how to behave socially after spending two years isolated in a dark room where he wrote his novel.

It is surprising that the Oprah producers, in their background checks of participants in their programs, overlooked Franzen's essays, particularly the 1998 "Imperial Bedroom," and his hostile statements about the shamelessness of television. They may have earlier realized that Franzen's and Oprah's philosophies are less than compatible. Longing to return to a time when public and private worlds were separate, Franzen is no more sanguine about cell phones than the fare on television. He is disturbed by the technological, mass-produced existence we lead, where real books, that is, literature, have been replaced by computers.

In his introductory essay, "My Father's Brain," about the deterioration of his father from Alzheimer's disease, and the penultimate essay, "Meet Me in St. Louis," about the Oprah connection, a reader may find glimpses into the writer's inmost being, sad and sensitive not only about his own issues but also those of modern life. He cannot bear to have outsiders probe into his private world apart from what he is willing to reveal. How then would anyone, including Franzen, have thought he could be a candidate for any television program that thrives on the personal and intimate? No wonder, early on, he found himself "failing as an Oprah author."

There are two entertaining addenda to the whole matter: one is a statement from Franzen's editor at Farrar, Straus, and Giroux, who pointed out the "silver lining" to Oprah's cancellation of the author's appearance on her show, which significantly increased sales. The other is that *The Corrections* won the fifty-second National Book Award. At the dinner, with actor and comedian Steve Martin as host for the third time, Franzen thanked Oprah. It should be noted, however, that the story lingers on.

Not many authors are reluctant to become known to the public, particularly when their books, no matter how well written, significant, or appealing, would more often than not have a limited audience. Given the thousands of books published each year, wide readership is like a game of chance. Furthermore, even with strong reviews, many books fail to attract attention from prospective readers. Works of nonfiction, apart from politics or history, have more of an uphill fight to reach large audiences. Not all of the books Oprah periodically singles out are novels, nor have they been works discussed by the book club. For a number of years, Oprah has selected nonfiction publications to discuss on her program. One such book, for instance, was Rachel Simmons's *Odd Girl Out: The Hidden Culture of Aggression in Girls*.

Rachel Simmons appeared on Oprah's show to talk about her book along with her friend, Rosalind Wiseman. Also an author, Wiseman had written *Queen Bees and Wannabes: Helping Your Daughter Survive Cliques, Gossip, Boyfriends, and Other Realities of Adolescence*, which was the impetus for the movie *Mean Girls*. They discussed the subject of both books, aggression among adolescents, a topic that interests Oprah and that has been discussed in her magazine, *O*. Oprah has told interviewers that she was a victim of bullying and aggression throughout her childhood and during her college days.

Simmons, a member of an organization called "The Ophelia Project," designed in conjunction with others, including psychologists, curricula dealing with antibullying techniques and relational aggression. The organization trains high school mentors to inculcate in young girls skills to face and prevent assertive behavior from others. They and similar groups work with both young boys and girls to teach them about boundaries, as well as control of relationship arguments and violence. One tenet of these programs is also a constant topic in Oprah's speeches and writing, that everyone, male and female, young and old, has to learn that our lives are in our own hands. We cannot bypass either hurtful situations or the person who causes suffering; the person who has given us pain or made us angry must be made aware of the issue. It is essential to assess our own feelings and if necessary get help from those around us whom we like and trust so that we are enabled to speak out. When we allow fear of loss to prevent us from being open and honest we can only lose more. Simmons, and Oprah, have said that readers and listeners must take charge of their own lives. The subject is one that resonates in all the interviews that Oprah gives.

In urging girls and women to refrain from expressing anger or aggressiveness, our culture has always taught dishonesty, and this behavior must change. If openness in relationships means being cast out by friends or groups, the experience may lead to "more centered, authentic self-awareness," says Simmons. We may be able to find other people who feel as we do, and, when we discover them, life will get easier.

In rethinking the matter of the book club, less than 10 months after her decision to abandon the entire concept, Oprah surprised viewers and the book-reading public at the end of February 2003 with an announcement that was reminiscent of the late comedienne Gilda Radner's humorous line, "never mind." It made newspaper headlines in both the "hard" news and style/entertainment sections: Oprah was reviving her book club. But instead of proclaiming that she'd found current books all right, worthy of reading and discussing after all, she said that she was going to rediscover the classics. She would now read the great writers of the past: Shakespeare, Faulkner, and Hemingway, among others. While being honored with a standing ovation for all she had previously done to inspire an interest in current books, she told the Association of American Publishers that she would again recommend books, "but with a difference." To speculation about whether her decision would bring the same kind of joy as her announcement of the formation of the original book club, the consensus at the time was: "Not likely." Publishing, like other industries, thrives on sales, and publishers were unsure whether they would make money on these old classics when people could simply dust off old copies of these books or find them at the library. Others questioned the appeal of books that readers associate with English classes in high school or college. However, it soon became clear that Oprah's name would be the drawing card again when she made her first choice for the reinstated club.

About her choice of the word "classic," Oprah told an interviewer, Michael Logan of *TV Guide*, that she was giving up applying that term to her selections; she wasn't anxious to engage in an argument with those critics she labels "the hoot-a-hahs of the literary world," and she changed the description of her chosen books to "great reads from the past." She says that the "overwhelming" reaction she felt reading John Steinbeck's *East of Eden* led her to reinstate the club.

The announcement of the revitalization of the club brought recognition from the hearts, pens, and programs of comedians and cartoonists. Columnists found some humor in the announcement of Oprah's "traveling with the classics."

Multiple writers, including British critic Christopher Hitchens, were unable to resist giving advice to Oprah. When he told a group of high school students that she should consider a discussion of Tolstoy's *Anna Karenina*, Hitchens playfully put forth the idea that it could provide material for a long, long time for Oprah and her friend psychologist Dr. Phil McGraw—Oprah has since followed his choice. Hitchens also recommended George Eliot's novel *Middlemarch*, which he said would be particularly appropriate for Oprah's show. The novel, which tells of the sexual and intellectual frustrations of an unhappily married Victorian woman, is one that, he said, would offer endless possibilities for Oprah's program.

So-called classics—or just "good reads from the past"—are having a revival of sales with Oprah's new undertaking, even if the authors are dead. It has become more difficult in recent years for current writers either to get published or to make any money from their writing, at least in America if they are not selected for special programs such as Oprah's and the *Today* show. Large foreign corporations control much of the book industry, and publication now has less to do with quality than marketability. A world-famous star with an international following can have a major impact on the reading public. When Oprah announced her choice of a so-called classic in June 2003 for the newly revived book club, Borders and Waldenbooks immediately were overwhelmed by sales of more than 5,000 paperback copies of a book written more than 50 years ago: John Steinbeck's *East of Eden*. The novel quickly became number one among paperback best sellers. According to Oprah, the book "may actually be better" than Steinbeck's most famous novel, *The Grapes of Wrath*, because it has everything from "love and betrayal and greed and murder and sex."

Television talk show host Oprah Winfrey puts her feet up as she relaxes in her studio office following a morning broadcast in Chicago, Ill., on December 18, 1985, a week before her movie debut in The Color Purple. *AP/Wide World Photos.*

Oprah Winfrey heads an all-star cast in the story of seven women seen over a period of several decades in The Women of Brewster Place. *© 1989 Capital Cities/ABC, Inc. Photofest, Inc.*

Oprah Winfrey surrounded by the cast of The Women of
Brewster Place, *prior to an encore presentation of the
show in 1990. © 1989 Capital Cities/ABC, Inc.
Photofest, Inc.*

*Oprah Winfrey at work shooting another installment of her talk show, first nation-
ally syndicated in 1986. © Harpo/Kingworld. Photofest, Inc.*

Kimberly Elise, Oprah Winfrey, and Thandie Newton in a shot from the movie
Beloved, produced by Oprah's own Harpo Films and released in 1998. © Touchstone
Pictures. Photofest, Inc.

Talk show host and actress Oprah Winfrey, recipient of the first Bob Hope Humanitarian Award at the 54th annual Emmy Awards September 22, 2002, in Los Angeles, relaxes with companion Stedman Graham at the Governor's Ball following the
show. © REUTERS NewMedia, Inc./CORBIS.

Chapter 5

INTIMATES

Although a woman of Oprah's prominence naturally has a wide variety of friends, colleagues, lovers, and acquaintances, four names surface most frequently: Maya Angelou, Gayle King (Bumpus, her former married name), Quincy Jones, and Stedman Graham. Each has had a different role in her life, and the feelings she has expressed about each range from simple, unconditional love to the complexities of uncertainty and indecision.

The oldest is Maya Angelou. Born in 1928, and almost 30 years older than Oprah, she would seem to represent more of a mother figure than a friend. And, in fact, Angelou has spoken of Oprah as the daughter she wishes she had. And Oprah has spoken of Angelou as both a dream mother and a wonderful friend, with a compatibility more satisfying than the maternal bond she had with Vernita Lee.

Poet, memoirist, dancer, actress, lecturer, and teacher (and in the distant past, waitress in a bar, pimp, fry cook, calypso singer, and composer of incidental music), Angelou has a unique place in American culture. She followed in the literary footsteps of Robert Frost, who in old age read a poem at the inauguration of John F. Kennedy in January 1961. Three decades later, a black woman poet, Maya Angelou, read her "love song," entitled "On the Pulse of Morning," at the first inauguration of William J. Clinton in January 1992. A group of actresses working with Angelou on the film *How to Make an American Quilt* labeled her an "icon." Much of the world would agree that Angelou is an icon, although the *Baltimore Sun*'s preferred label has been "Renaissance Woman."

The rather distancing word "icon," respectful as it is, might not be what Oprah herself would choose. It has the ring of a eulogy, akin to a term that

Professor Mary Lupton of Morgan State College applied to an interview with Angelou—"sacred." These are not the first things one would say of a dear friend, although it is obvious from her words and actions that Oprah regards Angelou as a powerful, even mythic figure. Every journalist writing about the connection between the two women calls Angelou Oprah's mentor. Yet, more than Angelou's status in the world of artists, black or white, has led to the close tie between the women. So many aspects of their individual histories link them. Ironically, even the inconsistencies of information about each are striking when we look at them. Statements, written as fact, yet differing in various interviews and biographies, casual remarks given over time, and the subject's changing memories of events are undoubtedly characteristic of biography in general, as they are of details about Angelou's and Oprah's histories. However, given the close relationship of the two women, anyone viewing them side by side cannot help but be struck by the multiple similarities of their lives past and present. Oprah's and Angelou's early histories reflect, at many points, those of black women in America, a point Oprah has made often over the years.

Both women have had more than one name, a subject that has been a source of interest to biographers. Angelou started out as Marguerite Annie but early on became "Maya," the name conferred by her brother as a combination of "my" and "my sister." She later dropped her last name, Johnson. Finally, after a divorce, she took the stage name used in her night club appearances—Angelou—the designation that stuck. Oprah has had fewer names, though no less intriguing. Oprah's strong and inspirational Aunt Ida, was the person who wanted to give her the biblical name Orpah. Her name became Oprah, and the baby was also given a middle name, Gail, a name by which she was and still is known by various people. Yet a third name is associated with Oprah: Harpo, an amusing, yet not intentional reminder of the comic Marx brother. However, the name of Oprah's production company comes from Oprah spelled backwards. Angelou's parents had been married, and her family name came from her father Bailey Johnson; but Oprah, born to the unmarried Vernita Lee, was given the last name of Winfrey, yet has never been completely certain about her paternity. In spite of her strong feelings of loyalty and duty toward Vernon Winfrey, she has pointed out, sometimes humorously, that she bears no resemblance to him and that her mother had a record of promiscuity.

Both Angelou and Oprah were separated at an early age from their mothers, who were unable or unwilling to care for them. Both children stayed with their strong and stern grandmothers for several years before going to live with their mothers in other cities. Unfortunately, the two mothers were alike in their indifferent care for their children, and each girl was sent elsewhere again, Maya back to her grandmother, and Oprah to her father and stepmother for a short time before her mother insisted on her return. In the homes of their mothers nobody supervised their lives; boyfriends and or male relatives came and went, and the laxity of the households led to the sexual abuse of both little girls. Each one was raped, Angelou, at the age of eight by her mother's boyfriend, Oprah, at nine, by a much-loved cousin who shared her bed in a relative's over-crowded apartment where sexual abuse was ignored or overlooked. Their early years were marked by predatory males who had no compunctions about violating the children. Although today Oprah seems more scarred than Angelou by the experience, Angelou was so traumatized as a little girl that she did not speak for several years.

As teenagers both girls became mothers; Angelou was 16 when she gave birth to her son Guy as the result of a sexual relationship with a neighborhood boy. Oprah at 14 gave birth to an illegitimate son, father unknown; however, unlike Angelou's son, her child did not live. The episode was kept secret for many years until Oprah's hostile and jealous half-sister revealed the experience to the press. Oprah would not speak to her sister for two years after that incident. In maturity, however, both Angelou and Oprah are candid about the suffering of their early years, Angelou in her writing and Oprah in her television programs. Nevertheless, in spite of their disastrous sexual experiences in childhood, both have gone on to other relationships with men, happy and unhappy, though Angelou sounds more philosophic about them. A number of failed marriages and liaisons have not interfered with what she openly calls her enjoyment of men. But she also has made it clear in her writings that she has not allowed sex to be the governing factor of her life. On the other hand, Oprah has never married and has confessed to several interviewers the pain that sexual domination brought into her life, from her teens right through her years in Baltimore when an affair with a married man brought her close to suicide.

On television, nevertheless, Oprah usually—though not always—has been less personal and less serious in many of her discussions about sex; the exceptions have to do with matters of abuse involving children and disclosure of the sexual abuse she suffered as a child and teenager, a subject she continues to discuss, decades later, in the few interviews she grants. In her magazine, she has stated that her determination to bring about change in the lives of girls comes from her own suffering. In other instances on her program, she employs humor to deflect from the private revelation. Thus, not infrequently, the external and social Oprah laughingly makes audacious statements about sexual matters; just about every biographer has picked up her televised comments about the pleasure of penis size, and her seemingly innocent question to prostitutes about "soreness" resulting from frequent and multiple sexual encounters. No less open and humorous, though not usually quoted, have been her television comments about the enjoyment of rolling around in bed. Clearly her audience relishes such utterances as if she were putting on a late-night comic show. Of course, Oprah's treatment depends on the nature and profundity of the television program, but her attitude toward sex, that sex is a good part of life, resembles that of Angelou. Oprah's statements are earthy, but less gentle and warm, not filled with the charm of the poet, who, even in age, speaks of the racing of her heart and her "luck" in having a lover even in her seventies.

Because of their different experiences, Angelou appears to be more forgiving of the past than Oprah. Yet, Oprah was fathered by a moral, upright man, determined to see his daughter become an achiever, whereas Angelou's parents, her handsome deadbeat father and beautiful indifferent mother, had no part in her ultimate success. Given the undependability of her mother, described by writer Hilton Als as "feckless," and "hard," a hot-tempered gin drinker, whom "many men found irresistible," Angelou's tolerance seems surprising. In fact, her writings suggest that the past made her the vital, complete woman she became. Although both women suffered greatly in their childhood, most often the result of the indifference of their weak, absent, and self-involved mothers, Angelou's absolution appears to have been total by the end of her mother's life. Oprah's financial generosity to her mother and other members of her family is well known, yet remarks she has made over the years intimate that there are still unresolved issues, in spite of the fact that numerous members of her family are now dead. Where Angelou speaks freely of the discovery of the depth of her love for her mother, Oprah does not make such a claim, although at times she has spoken of forgiveness for the woman entrapped from youth in an unforgiving world.

Angelou seems the more insouciant of the two, not reluctant to give advice to Oprah. In a humorous variation on the so-called certainty in each life of death and taxes, Angelou pointed out her version of the only inevitabilities: death and color. Suggesting to the younger woman that she slow down, she has also acknowledged and admired the "dizzying pace" that Oprah has set for herself. Whether Oprah can take such advice only the future will tell, although on several occasions she has made public statements about future plans to give up several of her activities, the most significant of which is her television show. However, inevitably she retracts her statements.

Oprah often takes a leaf from Angelou's journey as she honors publicly the life of African Americans. Typically, in 1989, speaking to the National Council of Negro Women, with language as poetic as that of her friend Maya, she focused on celebrating the histories of blacks throughout history, as well as the terrible, wonderful, inspirational journey they have taken throughout time. Although Angelou seems to feel more connectedness to slavery as a result of her more varied experiences—including time spent in Africa—in their lives and work both women have identified with that grim past in America and elsewhere. Even though Angelou has spoken more often than Oprah of black history, Oprah also regards herself as part of the continuum. In conversation with interviewers, and in remarks on television, she talks of her gratitude for her grandmother's influence, identifying with the many, many black children who were raised or taken care of by grandmothers and other relatives in the absence of parents.

So warm is the relationship between Oprah and Angelou that Oprah has paid homage to the older woman's birthday several times in great style. In 1993 she threw a sixty-fifth birthday party for Angelou, a social gathering said to rival only Truman Capote's "Black and White Ball." Spoken of as the definitive party of the 1970s, Capote's ball honored Katherine Graham after the completion of his book *In Cold Blood*. His party was held in New York, where for a brief time Capote was king, with a court consisting mostly of whites. Angelou's party, while not given the amount of publicity of Capote's, nevertheless rivals it. The celebration was held on the grounds of the conference center at Wake Forest in Winston-Salem, the city where Angelou lives and works. Guests at the party spoke of the elegant catering, the decorations, and the special food and drinks, as well as the major highlight—greetings by satellite from President Clinton. In her magazine, Oprah has described this and the other parties she has thrown for Angelou.

The invitees, famous as well as lesser-known people, flown in from various parts of the world for the festivities, were predominantly black, as are a large number of people in Oprah's inner circle. Yet Oprah has not always fared well among various members of the black population, including those who protested in North Carolina as a result of the publicity she gave to a white section of Winston-Salem. She had been jogging not far from

Angelou's home, and happened to see a beautiful home owned by white people, met the family, and later publicized pictures of their house. Although the publicity made Angelou unhappy, this was not the first time that members of the black community have spoken out about Oprah: they have boycotted her movies and opposed programs they found objectionable.

Aside from their party giving, it is an interesting footnote to history to recognize there are some similarities in the early days of Angelou, Oprah, and Capote—the abandonment, sense of loss, and misery that each child, black or white, faced. In fact, Angelou, in her collection of essays *Wouldn't Take Nothing for My Journey Now*, calls attention to the link to Capote when she describes a trip she took to New Orleans. There, with the openness and empathy that marks her, and with a play on the title of Capote's first novel, she speaks of "the other places and rooms" of Truman Capote's "torturous childhood," tipping her hat, in a sense, to all the children whose lives have been blighted. Oprah, on the other hand, generally appears to focus more on children of color.

Angelou's celebration of their friendship may be seen in her dedication to Oprah in that same 1993 collection, *Wouldn't Take Nothing for My Journey Now*, though the book contains nothing about Oprah except the dedication declaring "immeasurable love." Oprah's own immeasurable love is returned in numerous ways. For instance, Oprah has publicized Angelou's book, *A Song Flung Up to Heaven*, the sixth and final volume in her autobiography. An excerpt, "I Have Come to Collect You," appeared in the April 2002 edition of the magazine O. Excerpts also appeared elsewhere, although critics, charmed as they are by Angelou herself, pointed out—gently—that this latest book was not her best.

Hilton Als, however, in evaluating the body of Angelou's work, and concluding with a critique of *A Song Flung Up to Heaven*, finds that Angelou does not really belong in the place some critics have assigned her, with "her politically minded contemporaries." Instead, he places her among those interested in self-revelation, "theatrical writers...who describe and glorify a self that is fulfilled only when it is being observed." Perhaps most people in the entertainment business have that trait. Author Barbara Grizzuti Harrison has stated that "celebrities need one another—they ratify one another's myths. They are one another's truest fans."

Once a nominee for a Pulitzer Prize in poetry in 1971, Angelou now writes epigrams, that is, inspirational thoughts, for Hallmark. In spite of her fame, she seems to take to heart Poet Laureate Billy Collins's view that such writing is "tacky." With a statement that sounds extremely defensive, she tells reviewer/interviewer Linton Weeks of the *Washington Post* that Collins doesn't like her.

Perhaps. But large numbers of people do like her, and Oprah, among them, revels in the friendship. Another instance of the warmth of that relationship is reported in the May 2002 issue of *O*. Following the announced theme of the month, "Fun," Oprah tells of the seventieth birthday celebration she held for Maya Angelou in an essay entitled "The Most Fun I Ever Had." This time it was a week's cruise to the Mayan ruins in Tulum, Mexico, for Angelou and 70 of her oldest friends. Oprah was playful in her planning: Mayan for Maya, and 70 friends for her age. A year's careful thinking had gone into the production of the "blast," filled with all kinds of imaginative happenings.

In writings that Angelou calls her "thoughts" and the editors call a "continuation," Angelou published, in 1997, another set of essays. There, in *Even the Stars Look Lonesome*, Angelou pays tribute to Oprah with "Poetic Passage," a four-page profile of her friend/daughter. Characteristically, Angelou begins with a description of three types of travelers: the extremely careful and prudent one; the easily defeated and disappointed one; and the bold, vulnerable one. These three metaphorically are journeying through life; among them is Oprah in the most difficult group, the third. The "baggage" she has carried—poverty, the powerlessness of color and gender—has not interfered with her journey. In fact, says Angelou, Oprah has been both "conductor and porter," the one who has carried her own baggage. In words of great praise, the writer directs our attention to the complexities that make up Oprah, the little girl and the woman, the one who sinned yet has "a genuine fear of sin"; the believer in goodness, the empathetic "would-be sister" to many of thousands of the people she meets.

Among the many guests at Angelou's seventieth birthday celebration was Quincy Jones, the man Oprah names as the first person in her life to teach her the meaning of love, the person who made her feel purposeful. If he were to die, she declares, she would weep for the rest of her life. The depth of her affection for Jones becomes even more evident in the connection she makes between Jones and her spiritual side, frequently describing him as a man who "walks in the light." More than that, Oprah has said in interviews, she wrote in her journal many years ago that Quincy "is the light." With humor, Jones tells the reader of his autobiography that he wears a sweatshirt proclaiming Oprah's unconditional love for him, which means he "can never fuck up." Although, he is less sentimental—or outspoken in his affection and admiration for Oprah, clearly, Quincy Jones also loves her.

The much-repeated story of their meeting appears in greater or lesser detail in various places, including O. Oprah calls their meeting "providential." In 1985, when Oprah hosted the show, A.M. *Chicago*, the forerunner of her *Oprah Winfrey Show*, she and Jones hadn't met. Although she had read Alice Walker's *The Color Purple* and knew that it was going to be made into a film, she had no link to the people who were casting, directing, or producing it. Like many other readers of Walker's novel, she was so much entranced by the story that she dreamed of having some part in the movie. But what happened seems like a story in itself. Quincy Jones was in Chicago briefly to testify in a lawsuit on behalf of Michael Jackson. At that time Jones, along with the young Steven Spielberg, was to be co-producer of the film made from Walker's Pulitzer Prize–winning novel, for which casting was underway. While sitting in his Chicago hotel room, Jones happened to turn on the television set, where he saw Oprah's show, which was not yet the nationally syndicated powerhouse it would later become. So strong was the effect on him that he immediately was convinced he'd found the woman to play Sofia in the film. The rest is movie history. Oprah's skills had been honed since childhood, and, as Jones has pointed out in his *Autobiography*, Oprah was not a novice but someone with a background of 15 years as a broadcaster. So she was prepared for the next step, and, during her October 2001 interview with him for O magazine—the theme was "Intimacy"—he recalls her philosophy about luck as "opportunity meeting preparation." Oprah has made the statement so frequently that it has been reported in multiple places, although critics point out that this idea of luck is in direct conflict with her view of destiny. She is sometimes censured by those critics for trying to have it both ways—ways that are polar opposites.

Jones also notes that the famed actor, Sidney Poitier—the first black to receive an Academy Award, and a man honored by the Academy in March 2002 with a Lifetime Achievement Award—regards Oprah as "a miracle," a woman with both "a gift and a mission." As for Oprah, on a number of occasions she has declared that the happiest day of her life came when Spielberg notified her she was his choice to play the role of Sofia in *The Color Purple*. She has always said that acting is what she loves most, but the television show brings in a steady income, allowing her to do the things she wants in her life. Even though the film had a mixed reception among critics and audiences, causing much anger, even outrage among black men, many critics consider it to be one of the better films of the decade. Unique in numerous ways with its examination of race and the relationships between black men and women, the book and movie also look openly at matters that were generally hidden behind walls of secrecy: physical and sexual abuse, and incest. For Oprah, however, the unexpected response was her first encounter with a large number of angry, hostile males. In some areas large numbers of people picketed or denounced the film. Stung by some of the attacks, Oprah defended the film and its subject matter, emphasizing that women, not men, were the focus. As noted previously, this would not be the last time that her work and position were criticized, for, as her career advanced, she tackled many other controversial subjects in her television programs, in movies, and in miniseries made for television.

The Color Purple won 11 nominations for the Academy Award, including one for Oprah as best supporting actress; yet neither the picture nor Oprah came away with an award. Even now, after all his successes, Jones recalls his feelings of devastation when the film failed to garner any of the awards. However, the friendship forged between Jones and Oprah has continued over the years. In that same interview in the October 2001 issue of her magazine, Oprah's remarks at times are worshipful, at times bantering, but always affectionate. She jokes about Jones's large number of marriages—five—after telling him they are going to speak only of important loves, that is, "just the top ten!" In Oprah's comparison of their two backgrounds, the printed interview captures the tonal quality of the quick wit apparent in her television personality: she was poor, she states, when she lived with her grandmother, but Jones and his family were "po'!" Oprah's audience knows that her grandmother served food made almost entirely from her farm's homegrown vegetables—and fried everything else, whereas Q, a city child, recalls, in his *Autobiography*, his grandmother had to fry rats along with collard greens for family meals. His deprivation resembles experiences in the childhood of many of Oprah's friends, as well as popular entertainers. On her television show, Oprah will refer to those instances, sometimes seriously, sometimes humorously. When she and a guest, comedian Bernie Mac, talked of his impoverished youth, Oprah showed clips of the broken-down neighborhood in which he'd lived. Mac, however, lightened the discussion by describing his family as so hard up and their apartment so dilapidated that the roaches moved out when they moved in.

Many things reveal the closeness of Oprah's and Jones's relationship in important and unimportant ways. Her admiration for him has been so evident for years, that she, a so-called media empress, seemed an obvious

choice to be his presenter as an honoree at the Kennedy Center Honors
Gala in December 2001. Although *Washington Post* reporter Paul Farhi
described the gala as "looney," "supremely hokey," and a highbrow "carni-
val," the annual event carries great prestige. At the gala and elsewhere,
Oprah's regard for Quincy Jones appears limitless. Reporters recall
Oprah's saying that Jones outranks almost everyone in kindness and gen-
erosity. Supporting that view, Oprah singled Jones out for her Angel
Award, which reads: "In Recognition of Commitment to Encouraging
Normal, Positive, and Healthy Attitudes Toward Sexual Relationships
Between Young Adults."

Quincy Jones also appeared a year later, in the September 2002 issue of
O, in which the theme is "Dream Big." One of the articles, entitled "Healing: The Day That Shook Our World," contained 11 short pieces about
the aftermath of September 9, 2001. With a subtle emphasis on the word
"eleven," the issue included reflections by 11 well-known Americans.
People from the print and television news media and the film, entertainment, and literary world wrote of the changes in their thinking as a result
of the national catastrophe. Every view was personal and each is different
from all the others.

Jones was one of the writers featured in that issue of the magazine. His
view was part of three headlines that served as an introduction to the collection of articles. Jones spoke of his early days in music when, as a trumpet player, he traveled with music star Lionel Hampton in 1953, the year
before Oprah was born. Jones also went with Dizzy Gillespie in 1956 to
North Africa and to countries that have become familiar names to us
since then: Syria; Lebanon; Pakistan, then a rather young country; and
Iran, whose later revolutionary overthrow of its government and adoption
of strict fundamentalist laws provided the world with an introduction to
religious upheavals in the Moslem world. Revolution was in the air, Jones
told us, so strong it could be smelled and felt through the music, and even
though the events of September 11 were horrific, they had been building
over the decades. As he has done before, Jones made a plea for harmony
and the understanding that can come when we recognize that intense
poverty in a third of the world leads to the type of disasters we have wit-
nessed.

In the October 2001 issue Oprah wrote both humorously and senti-
mentally about her relationship with Jones. On the lighter side, she told
of being a guest in his home, where she *actually* used his towels and ate the
fantastic spareribs he grills—all these details to emphasize fun as an addition to the solidity of their connection. Although she didn't mention it in

her interview of Jones, he was the man Oprah invited to escort her to a dinner party given by President and Mrs. Clinton at the White House for the Japanese Emperor and Empress. Reporters took note of it, speculating about reasons for her failure to ask her longtime boyfriend, Stedman Graham to accompany her. Whatever Oprah has said about that choice, the reasons for it remain a matter of conjecture. Although on another visit to the White House, Graham was her date, Oprah continues to appear with Jones on many a prestigious occasion.

When Oprah attends an event, more often than not she, as well as the event, is covered in the news. Thus, when Halle Berry won the Academy Award for best actress in *Monster's Ball* in 2002, Oprah, who was one of many celebrities at an awards party, was written up in the newspaper briefs. Berry, making movie history as the first black woman given the award, listed in her acceptance speech long lists of people who had helped or influenced her in her road to stardom. Among them was Oprah, on whose show Berry had appeared only a few days earlier. When Berry called Oprah her "role model," Oprah, watching the show at the *Vanity Fair* party with other notables, was visibly moved. Most of the postawards stories focused on the clothing and hairdos of the rich and famous attendees rather than the personal and moving details; though the large audience, including the people singled out by Berry, cheered and cried at her selection, the news briefs typically singled out Oprah, printing a photo of her along with a few lines describing her as someone who had broken down with tears. Oprah's tears and those of others that night of the awards were tears of joy over the historic break in the color barrier. Over the years few black people have been present on Oscar night; every step forward has been a triumph: the larger presence of African Americans at the ceremonies, the night that Oprah herself was a presenter of an award, and the win by Berry. Berry and Oprah remain close friends, although Berry is much younger.

Whether Berry has made a significant change for women of color remains to be seen, but almost immediately following the awards she was shown filming a new James Bond movie, *Die Another Day*, with Pierce Brosnan. The success of the Bond film following immediately on her winning the Oscar guarantees Berry some longevity in films. Also, in late 2003, Oprah told an interviewer that she is working on a film based on Hurston's novel *Their Eyes Were Watching God*, with Halle Berry playing the lead character Janie.

Although at times Oprah has said that her friends are the people she works with on a daily basis, other interviews contradict that somewhat.

She has a number of friends, all from the larger world of entertainment, whose friendship with her has extended over the years. One such friend is Barbara Walters, the longtime television superstar of interviewing. Even though Donahue was the rival Oprah hoped to challenge for domination of talk shows, Walters was the person whom she wanted to emulate when she first took her job in Chicago; Diane Sawyer is another old friend, television superstar as newswoman/interviewer of a magazine show, and later coanchor of a popular morning show; and another of Oprah's friends of more than 20 years is television newswoman, Maria Shriver, daughter of Eunice Shriver Kennedy; their relationship began when both worked for WJZ-TV in Baltimore. Along with many people familiar to readers of society columns, Oprah was a guest at the marriage of Shriver to Arnold Schwarzenegger in 1986 in Hyannis, Massachusetts, where numerous members of the Kennedy clan were present, including Jackie Kennedy Onassis, widow of President John Kennedy. Oprah, invited to be part of the wedding ceremony, reputedly discussed with Mrs. Onassis the presentation of the poem she was going to read, Elizabeth Barrett Browning's "How Do I Love Thee?"

Through a number of the Chicago years yet another Baltimore connection continued with Debra DiMaio, who was an assistant producer for Oprah's WJZ-TV program when they became friendly, each one admiring the hard work of the other. DiMaio was a longtime friend as well as staff member. At the time that Oprah was thinking of a change of jobs, uncertain about programs or city, DiMaio was also searching for a higher rung on the job ladder. Ambitious and eager to find television work that offered more exposure, money, and prominence, both women had similar goals. DiMaio, however, left Baltimore first, to become the producer of a Chicago morning show called *A.M. Chicago*. Although the job promised multiple rewards for the young producer, disaster loomed when a competing station brought in the *Donahue Show*, and the host of *A.M. Chicago* decided to go elsewhere. At that point DiMaio's future did not look auspicious.

Fate, however, intervened to assist DiMaio and open the doors for Oprah when Dennis Swanson, the station manager of WLS-TV, began to search anxiously for a replacement to host the morning show. DiMaio decided there was an opportunity to salvage her job if she could interest the station manager in Oprah. Because DiMaio had used tapes of the Baltimore program when she applied for the job in Chicago, the tapes also served as an introductory audition for Oprah, and Swanson asked her to come to Chicago for a further audition. Impressed by Oprah's open, up-front style, Swanson offered her a four-year contract as well as more money than she'd been earning in Baltimore. When Oprah expressed concern about racism in the city and her own body image, the dynamic Swanson brushed aside her worries about the possibility of the Chicago audience's reaction. He was as certain as DiMaio that Oprah would be a winner, and both of them were proved right very quickly. Over a period of years Swanson moved up the corporate ladder of television, becoming president of WNBC-TV in New York, but he still says that he remembers with fervor his early meetings with Oprah. Diffident as she was about the possibility of her success, he saw in her what DiMaio had seen and what future audiences would soon discover. Here was a woman others could identify with, someone like their friends and neighbors.

DiMaio stayed with Oprah through a number of years, moving up with her as she went from local to national coverage to international star, and many people credit DiMaio for playing a large role in Oprah's success. Believing that destiny had brought them together, she supported Oprah not only because of the prospective star's own talents but also because she believed in Oprah's abilities. Always concerned about Oprah's image, it was DiMaio who could speak to her about excessive weight, but she also understood that much of the audience identified with the weight problem, as well as issues with men. The very facts of Oprah's difficult childhood, when she lived in poverty and suffered sexual abuse, revealed in the early years of her show the defenselessness of a woman who, on the surface, had everything; but according to the producer, Oprah's open, comfortable relationship with the audience helped build her confidence as well as the program from the very beginning.

DiMaio was the person who hosted Oprah's fortieth, plush, elegant birthday party in Los Angeles. But by 1994 DiMaio's so-called take-no-prisoners style had begun to cause multiple problems among other members of the company; complaints became more frequent and vociferous, with the result that Oprah, in spite of her stated belief in loyalty, decided to ask for DiMaio's resignation. Her actions, she maintained, were to preserve harmony in her company, yet critics of Oprah and her methods of operation believe that she had sanctioned DiMaio's tough management style knowingly because it allowed her to stand above the fray. Oprah, who had regarded DiMaio as both friend and colleague, recognized what she considered to be DiMaio's outstanding talent, by rewarding her through the years with generous presents; they included a six-carat diamond bracelet at one point, and later a carte blanche monthly certificate for every month throughout the year for dinners with friends in any city in the world. This last tribute came shortly before Oprah asked for her friend's resignation. However, DiMaio got a generous multimillion-dollar settlement package when she left. Oprah has insisted, in spite of denigration of her management style, that she did not use DiMaio as the vehicle to control problems. When *TV Guide* in 1994 labeled DiMaio as "dictatorial and icy," Oprah defended her, insisting she was not a dictator.

Oprah's generosity to members of her staff is well known. She has given expensive gifts, trips, and large bonuses, and picked up the entire cost for special occasions such as weddings. One producer, Mary Kay Clinton, is so attached to Oprah that she told an interviewer she "would take a bullet for her." Oprah was a maid of honor at the wedding of Mary Kay in 1988. Clinton, her husband, and eight-year-old daughter were among the small number of guests at an early Christmas dinner party publicized and photographed for O's December 2002 issue. The party was held on Oprah's farm in Indiana. Clinton's daughter Katy Rose, who is Oprah's godchild, was the only youngster in the group that also included Oprah's father and his second wife, Barbara, Gayle King, and Stedman Graham.

Not every member of the staff has fared as well as DiMaio and other favorites; there have been some unpleasant resignations and even a lawsuit, followed by so-called revelations about Oprah's form of management. One former producer even went online to complain about Oprah and her methods. As a result of various operational problems, Oprah decided to reorganize her company in the mid-nineties to institute better and tighter supervision. After speaking to people she trusted, she got advice from her good friend, Bill Cosby, who warned her that she needed to oversee her finances, which meant writing the checks herself. Another friend, Barbra Streisand, suggested that she have everyone who works for her sign privacy agreements. Having followed through on what experience taught others, Oprah runs a tight ship. The result of following Streisand's advice is that all information concerning Oprah's operations is very limited and centrally controlled. Confidentiality is strongly pursued in all of Oprah's undertakings. Even guests on her show or their families will not share information with outsiders, no matter how innocuous.

Surprising as it may seem, considering that she is a guest at many different types of parties and other events, Oprah has claimed at various times that she doesn't make friends easily, and it is obvious that those who are closest have been her intimates for years. One such person, her friend and colleague with whom Oprah has never been at odds, the woman she says that she loves above all others and speaks of again and again, is Gayle King. Oprah always refers to her as "best friend" and confidante. Oprah's enthusiastic approach to friendship and much of her life is apparent in words such as "best," "happiest," "for sure," "first," or "most," terms she also uses when she speaks of people such as Angelou, Jones, and King. Like many of her valued connections, the one with Gayle King goes back 25 years, to the days when both were working in Baltimore. Unlike Oprah, Gayle came from Maryland, where she had grown up in a middle-class family, her mother a housewife, her father an educated professional man. When the two women met, Gayle was still living with her mother in Chevy Chase, Maryland. Although Gayle, a production assistant, admired Oprah in her role as anchorwoman, they didn't really know each other until nature intervened; a winter storm prevented Gayle's driving the long distance home that night, and Oprah invited her to stay at her Columbia apartment just outside of Baltimore. When Oprah tells the story in O and elsewhere, as always, her sense of humor enters into it. According to her version, it was a matter of clean panties, which she had available or that she and Gayle could buy. No need to go 40 miles to get them. When friendship was the theme of O in August 2001, Oprah discussed her relationship with Gayle in the column, "What I Know for Sure." In the column, Oprah details the warmth and depth of affection she and Gayle have for each other.

Their lives are entwined in multiple ways, both in friendship and business. They speak daily, often several times, sharing the intimacies of the years—happiness as well as disappointments. Both note that Oprah was present for all the important occasions of Gayle's life, her wedding, the birth of her children, and her divorce. "Cheerleader" is the term Oprah uses for Gayle, the person who has seen her through successes and failures, through what Oprah calls her own "twisted and messed-up" relationships of younger days. Gayle is the booster and the practical one, the "nicest person" Oprah knows, the "better part of myself," attributing her own sense of stability, grounding, and centering to Gayle.

Although King has a separate life and interests of her own, with children and other family, she is also editor at large of the magazine. As far as the public is concerned, that role has not been defined, but her ties to Oprah in everything are clear. She is like a sister to Oprah. While in their twenties she was the designated recipient of the suicide note Oprah wrote, in Baltimore, while in the depths of despair over a failed love affair. Gayle has shared Oprah's fears and doubts about other relationships, including her longtime romance with Stedman Graham. Gayle served as public spokesman, through interviews, to squelch rumors about dalliances attributed to Stedman and unequivocally stated that Oprah has no reason to doubt her lover, that he never looks at other women. The particular impetus for the statement undoubtedly was a malicious rumor about Graham that circulated in a gossip column and aired on a show called *Entertainment Tonight*. The bizarre story held that Oprah had found Graham in bed with her hairdresser and shot him. The story was never substantiated. The *Chicago Sun-Times* discontinued the column in which the story had appeared, and on her television program Oprah passionately denounced the story as fabrication without telling the puzzled audience what it was all about. Her performance brought kudos from commentators and added to her reputation for restraint, poise, and dignity. Since that time, over the years, Oprah has schooled herself to publicly ignore gossip of all kinds, cruel or otherwise, taking heed of Maya Angelou's warning that gossip is another form of poison. Where in the past she wanted to confront those who spread untrue stories about her, she now says that she feels secure enough and comfortable in herself to turn away, at least outwardly, from such destructive talk.

For much of her life, Oprah had looked for the perfect man. In Graham she has appeared to find him. Although their relationship dates back to the year they first met, in 1985; it has followed a rocky road on occasion. Yet their relationship has lasted far longer and been more important than any other romantic involvement of Oprah's. She often has spoken of him on her television show, where he also has appeared and declared his love for her.

Naturally, like any young girl during her high school and college years in Nashville, Oprah had several boyfriends; in her senior year of high school she and a boy named Anthony Otey had a fairly typical, girl/boy relationship described as "platonic," one filled with secret codes and love notes, which Oprah saved as mementos of her high school years. The romance ended once she entered Tennessee State College, where she met a student named William Taylor, with whom, at the age of 17, she fell passionately in love. Young as she was, she wanted to marry him, but her passion was not reciprocated. Taylor, who later became a mortician, was not interested in marrying her, a decision for which she has said she is very grateful today and which she also has said that she is certain he regrets.

During her time in Baltimore, Oprah had one happy romance followed by a devastating affair, an experience that drove her to the brink of suicide. The earlier relationship with a reporter named Lloyd Kramer brought her pleasure and a feeling of self-worth, but both came to an end when Kramer left Baltimore to take a job in New York. After his departure, she became involved for four years in an emotionally destructive experience with a married man. The effect on her was the complete opposite of what she'd had with Kramer, and she has said that she felt powerless to extricate herself from a cruel, abusive, and demeaning situation. Reflecting, in recent years, on those unhappy experiences and her lack of confidence, she described her younger self as a "doormat" who allowed men to dominate her very existence. However, once the affair ended she vowed she would never again give herself over to another person's control no matter how lonely her life might be. Later in her career some of these experiences influenced the selection of topics for her television programs and magazine.

Moving from Baltimore to Chicago was a drastic change for her in every way, but she says that she fell in love with the city almost immediately. Among the large cities she could have chosen, she picked Chicago because, she has said, she finds it more civilized than New York, and she was concerned that she would not be a member of the predominant minority group in Los Angeles. In moving to Chicago, she declared that at last she'd come home, that she'd found roots, even though she was aware of the city's racist reputation. Conscious of the fact that her fame has served as a protective coat for her that most other black people do not have, when she speaks of the racist color barriers ordinary black people face, she also points out that she too has been treated like a second-class citizen because of her color, when she has gone into shops where she was not recognized. When she first arrived, she has said, she had limited fame and few friends. She was an insecure and lonely young woman for a long time. She has described nights and holidays spent alone in Chicago. Neither was there any real romance. Then she met Stedman Graham, someone who filled the requirements she'd been seeking: tall, handsome, intelligent, the kind of man she had dreamed about. Not only does Oprah refer to him as gorgeous, but so do the tabloids, her audience, and interviewers. Yet, her sense of insecurity was so strong at the time they met that she was reluctant to date him at first, feeling that he was much more desirable than she. Graham, on the other hand, has said he felt uncertain himself as their relationship developed along with the phenomenal rise in her career. Further, some of her friends, including Mary Kay Clinton, have told interviewers that they worried about the connection, wondering if he cared for the woman or her celebrity and money, issues about which he is very sensitive. It has taken many years for Oprah to accept the fact that millions of people consider her beautiful, funny, charming, clever, and exciting; so much of her energy has been concentrated on concerns about her weight and fear that her money is what draws men and women to her.

She has said that, like most people, she wants to be loved for herself, not her fame, success, or fortune.

However, Oprah did overcome her qualms about dating Graham, who impressed her with his suave and gracious manner. On their first date he brought roses, took her to dinner, and, above all, paid attention to what she had to say. Not long afterward they became a couple. During the early years of their romance, marriage seemed imminent. Oprah spoke frequently about her admiration of his many appealing qualities: his kind and supportive behavior, his patience and sense of honor, his interest in helping her to be true to herself. Further, like her, he has a sense of humor. Oprah even tried to play golf even though she didn't like the game, wanting to share more of his interests, but she found that she much prefers shopping. Together they are involved in many important activities in their desire to do good, to help the poor, the needy, and their communities.

For several years Oprah declared she'd never lived with anyone, nor would she; however, their very diverse lives, careers, and distance became a greater and greater problem. Eventually, Graham, who, because of his business, had been living in High Point, North Carolina, relocated his work and moved into the Chicago apartment with Oprah.

Marriage was discussed openly and publicly, not only by Oprah but also by her friends, and, year after year, journalists write that the two would marry "soon," or "next year." At Angelou's sixty-fifth birthday party in 1993, the poet announced an Oprah/Stedman wedding as upcoming, and subsequently there were frequent reports that the event was being planned. But now, more than a decade after Angelou's declaration, many people doubt the two will ever marry. Even though he and his former wife, Glenda, have a daughter, Wendy, now grown and finished with college, it has been said, in the tabloids, that Graham wanted more children. Yet, if it is possible to trust any report in the tabloids, his current feeling is to leave decisions about children to Oprah. Conscious of all the complexities of her life, said the journalist, Graham wants her to determine whether she would accept a dramatic change. Oprah, who has never seemed particularly interested in motherhood, claims she wouldn't be a good mother, and that she is beyond the child-bearing years. To explain her reluctance about marriage—the story continues—she previously told people that Graham wants and deserves a traditional wife, something she could not be because her career takes up too much of her life. The article notes she gives one reason after another, such as her statement, in 1995, when she was 41, that the biological clock was against her. Just as the generally unreliable tabloid press periodically writes that a Winfrey/Graham marriage is in the planning stage, it has also reported that Oprah is considering marriage or ways to become a mother, either—as the tabloids put it—through fertilization of her eggs by Graham's sperm, or by the mixture of his sperm with the eggs of a surrogate mother.

Oprah frequently has declared her lack of interest in motherhood. She reiterated it to Diane Sawyer in May 2004 during an hour-long interview on *Prime Time*. Oprah explained then, as she has on numerous occasions, that she could not have nurtured children in Africa and elsewhere if she'd been a mother.

In the wake of several announcements of Oprah's decision to retire from her television show, another story in the gossip-driven news spoke of a decision for an elopement "soon" and once again of the couple's intentions to have children, either their own or adopted. Yet, none of the previous stories or another one about "Oprah's Test Tube Baby" came from the star herself or Graham. Considering the many promises, announcements, and speculations over the years, there seems little reason to expect any change. Oprah has said again and again she has no intentions of marrying. Still, nobody other than Oprah seems willing to rule out the possibility of marriage, particularly if there is even a grain of truth about any personal plans, as reported in the tabloids with some regularity.

Graham himself is different from Oprah in many, many ways. He avoids the limelight and, although he has written of his own problems, is described by others as completely comfortable in himself, a man who isn't intimidated by Oprah's money or fame. Nevertheless, he had to struggle to overcome some uneasiness, as he reports in his books. Unquestionably, he holds views frequently contrary to Oprah's. He is a very proper kind of man—he doesn't drink and, unlike Oprah, has never taken drugs. On a 1995 show, Oprah revealed the fact that she had smoked cocaine 20 years earlier. It is rumored—something Oprah denies—that Graham was so appalled by the sexual revelations in her once-planned autobiography that he persuaded her to abandon it.

Oprah provided various reasons for breaking her contract, but a large factor in her decision was that Graham felt the book should be more uplifting and inspirational, attitudes he stresses in his own writing and lecturing. Graham's opinion was one that rang true with Oprah; she had unquestionably become a more spiritual person in recent years. Even though she became a star with her outspoken, so-called shoot-from-the-hip confessional technique, in interviews, her magazine, and on her program, she talks more frequently with the passing years of her spirituality, as do friends and colleagues. In 1988, she even had what she called a spiritual reading summer. That her spirituality is not a recent acquisition may be seen in a statement made by one of the television show's producers when Oprah was 34. The producer spoke with deep feeling about the effect on her of Oprah's spirituality. Stedman Graham also refers to that element of her character, and in various ways Oprah seems to focus on and speak often of her spiritual interests. In general remarks and interviews she emphasizes that she is a believer, obedient to the call of God; yet, in spite of her strongly religious childhood years, she tells audiences hers is not a traditional Christianity, because she finds most denominations of the church too limiting.

Still, at unexpected moments on her program and in her magazine she refers to the power of her faith, of the prayers she utters, of her joy in listening to and singing spirituals. Immediately after the horrors of September 11, 2001, when she had a program entirely focused on music, she told her audience of her need to be touched by the healing power of spirituals and the solace they brought as she listened. In her magazine, general references to faith appear in many contexts. The 2002 Christmas issue of O featured articles about the search for faith, one of which was highlighted on the cover as "The Search for a Spiritual Home." The biographical story, by Beverly Donofrio, explicated the point with her theme: "They say that if you're looking for God, you've already found him." At various times throughout this and other issues of the magazine Oprah referred to her own spirituality, the needs of the soul, and the prayers she offers on a regular basis. Kindness and charity, also described in a Christmas issue as well as others, bring about moral beauty, a state to which she always seems to aspire. Like others in her role, she has the power to represent hopes, dreams, and deeds. Without doubt, she inspires her readers, television viewers and all types of audiences to reflect on their own acts of benevolence.

Oprah has said that she believes strongly in the personal satisfaction that comes with goodness, but she, as a wealthy woman, credits goodness for her financial success. Graham's view of success is less spiritual and seemingly more commercial, yet both of them are conventional capitalists. Nevertheless, having found a satisfactory niche in the business world, Graham, like Oprah, has said that he wants to do good, to be a man who helps raise up those in need. He does not speak explicitly of his own spirituality in the same way she does; he explains his hesitancy to do so as a matter of privacy, although one might question his perception given the large number of personal revelations in writing and personal appearances.

Regardless of what he shares with an audience, though, he is less outgo-ing, more controlled, more cautious than Oprah.

Although Graham and Oprah had unhappy early lives, they were dif-ferent. Her unmarried mother had other children, although her father did not have any other children. Graham's married parents produced six off-spring, of whom Stedman was the third child and second son. Born in Whitesboro, New Jersey, he was part of a family in which his two younger brothers were mentally disabled. Although he describes his boyhood home in Whitesboro as an all-black community founded by Congressman George White, his ancestor, he has also said race for him was an issue in the community—Graham was too light for some and not white enough for others. Although in time he was able to accept his background, he told Oprah and the readers of his books that his boyhood years were painful. In middle age, having achieved status as well as financial success, he has said that he sees Whitesboro differently. Recently, distressed by the deteriora-tion of the town, he helped create a group called "Concerned Citizens of Whitesboro," whose mission is the revitalization as well as the restoration of the area and hopes of the townspeople.

After leaving Whitesboro to continue his education, he was the only one of the Grahams to finish college. He graduated from Hardin-Simmons University with a degree in social work, although it was basket-ball and a sports scholarship that led the way, the path of sports that many young talented men from poor homes follow to find more rewarding lives than have other family members. In college he was cocaptain of the bas-ketball team and has called himself a top scorer. His hopes for a career in basketball brought only limited success, but he continued to play on a military team and as a member of the European professional basketball league when stationed in Germany during the three and a half years he was in the American army. His stint as a basketball player, though, later provided the athletic background for another part of his business career, director of Athletes Against Drugs.

While in the service, he earned a master's degree in education, a pro-gram that served him well during his several different jobs after he left the army. For a time he worked in Colorado as a guard in the federal depart-ment of corrections, going on from that to become the director of edu-cation at the United States Metropolitan Correctional Center in Chicago. In two of his books, *You Can Make It Happen: A Nine-Step Plan for Success* and *Build Your Own Life Brand,* he notes his current credentials again and again: chairman and CEO of an organization that does man-agement, marketing, and consulting for minority companies, as well as sports and entertainment firms; founder of Athletes Against Drugs; co-author and author of several books; member of several charitable and nonprofit boards; and adjunct university professor, teaching at North-western University.

During the early part of his career he began to work with the disadvan-taged and guide them to become part of the American mainstream. Hav-ing been molded by his own experiences and influenced by men who had achieved success in their lives and work, he too found the necessary de-termination to do the same, and now he says that he is committed to helping others find the right path. When he and Oprah first met during the 1980s, they were very different from what they are today, but each played a major role in bringing about change in the other. Just as he be-lieves he has helped Oprah emotionally, he credits her greatly for his per-sonal growth, in helping him to look back at the source of his pain, the difficult family situation and his need for perfection that would prove his worth. Perhaps because of the sorrows of their childhoods, Oprah asserts that each has the desire to help disadvantaged young people improve their lives.

Nonetheless, that harmony did not exist earlier in their relationship. As she moved toward world fame, he found he was becoming uncomfort-able and angry with their situation. He wrote, as part of his narrative tech-nique in his self-help books, that they had begun as an average couple, but with her ever-growing career, he saw himself as less than equal, a man who was regarded as Oprah's boyfriend rather than a person in his own right. When he complained that he was being heckled because of his connec-tion to her, she was unsympathetic. She wanted him to analyze his feel-ings of insecurity, and as he looked at himself he began to understand he had to change, just as their lives had changed. He says that he knew he could not follow the traditional male role if they were to remain together. With Oprah leading the way, he tells the reader of his books, he learned about self-examination as well as self-understanding.

Influenced by author and "guru" Marianne Williamson, Oprah says that she came to believe Williamson's theory that childhood suffering teaches us about protecting our hearts against further bruises. Oprah dis-covered that for herself more quickly than Stedman, because, he claims, she is relentless in her pursuit of self-analysis.

Also, contradictory of his assertion that he is very private are the fre-quent invocations of Oprah's name and activities. The dedications in his first book, *You Can Make It Happen*, are to both Oprah and his father, who died the year before publication. Later in the book Stedman speaks of his father affectionately, praising his strength and commitment to family, a man whose character led his son to prize honesty, perseverance, and determination. Stedman has adopted Oprah's belief that we take on the virtues of someone close to us after that person has died. Thus, he made a promise to his dead father: not only would he continue to care for the family but he would also follow his own dreams. To do that, he notes in all lectures and books, requires determination, which is, according to his philosophy, essential to success. He illustrates the point by recounting a funny episode involving Oprah. The athletic Graham was attempting to water ski one day as Oprah watched. Try as he might, he could not get up on the skis. Finally, at one point, Oprah prayed that God would "let him make it" up on the skis, so that they could "go home." The anecdote serves a dual purpose as an example of her humor and his iron will.

A later book, *Build Your Own Life Brand,* is dedicated to Oprah alone. The dedications of both books have a disconcerting sentimentality seldom seen in print. These are private thoughts made public, evoking all the earmarks of television. In *You Can Make It Happen,* he thanks Oprah for both "her influence" and trust. Only through her did he learn "true freedom" in his life. After expressing his gratitude to her for removing the emptiness from his heart, he dramatically declaims, "Let the journey continue." The dedication in *Build Your Own Life Brand* is an even more intimate declaration, in which he addresses Oprah, speaking of her "life brand" as a model, with achievements so great that only her heart is larger.

The theme of the entire book is one of consumption. Everything, he writes, is related to consumption. The identity of an individual is a brand, unique to that person. Who we are and the elements that have made us have become our brand. Like a brand, a product, we try to make an impression, reveal our special qualities, and sell ourselves. We must market our brand, states Graham, and throughout his book he presents examples of people who have been successful in marketing their brand, that is, themselves. Needless to say, Oprah is one of those individuals. So too does he list her close friends, Maya Angelou and Quincy Jones, plus one of his own close friends, the basketball star Michael Jordan whom he had interested in Athletes Against Drugs.

At times, it is unclear how far-reaching is his definition of brand. When he speaks about the media's taking "control" of his brand when he first dated Oprah and complains that his "true value" was ignored, the reader has difficulty in determining whether he is speaking of his credentials or his character, inasmuch as he appears to link the two together. His repetitive listing of his achievements, while intended to be inspirational to his readers and those who attend his seminars, sound defensive as he describes his many activities as belonging to "Success Circles." With his constant references to his activities and achievements, the reader is left with the impression that the books are more biographical than educational. Much of the writing seems to be self-praise clothed in the garments of self-help teaching.

Oprah does not publicly espouse affiliation to any political party, having never been involved with politics. She has appeared with both Democratic and Republican presidents, and she is more liberal-minded than is Graham. Their diverse political views often seem obvious in the type of affairs each attends. During the presidential campaign of 1996, for example, Graham went to Republican fund-raisers, such as the one given for candidate Steve Forbes, but he attended the party without Oprah. His business connections also point to conservatism. He was president of the Graham Williams Group, a public relations company. His partner in that venture, Armstrong Williams, once an assistant to Senator Strom Thurmond and then to Clarence Thomas prior to Thomas's appointment to the Supreme Court, is a well-known conservative. Today, Graham's books as well as the vita provided by a speaker's bureau list him both as chairman of Stedman Graham Training and Development and chief executive officer of Stedman Graham & Partners. The first company provides seminars and related services, and the second is a marketing agency.

His how-to books, numbered as 3 by the speaker's bureau, 15 by Barnes and Noble, and the bureau's somewhat vague and highly inflated descriptions of his speeches and seminars, focus entirely on ways to achieve success. A combination biography and self-help process, consisting of nine steps and inspirational messages are the central elements of his books and presentations. Motivational seminars appear to be extremely popular among his numerous topics for speaking engagements. However, one important, perhaps the most important element in his various presentations, is his premise that nobody needs to be a victim of his own history. That position is supported by his own life story and is a central pillar in Oprah's philosophy.

Gushingly described at different times and by different reporters from the *Washington Post* as "a commanding presence" and a "good-looking guy," Graham has been interviewed at length about some of his books, generally dubbed "inspirational." The titles, *You Can Make It Happen: A Nine-Step Plan for Success* and *You Can Make It Happen Every Day*, lend themselves to that designation. It is unsurprising, however, to learn that the real interest of interviewers is not in his books but in his lengthy romance with the television star. As Megan Rosenfeld, of the *Washington Post* describes it, the long engaged couple are similar to Runyon's *Guys and Dolls* characters, Nathan Detroit and Miss Adelaide, the biblical Jacob and Rachel, and Dickens's David Copperfield and his Agnes.

Graham has written numerous other books as well, each belonging to the category of inspirational, motivational, or self-help: in 1994, *Takeovers*; in 1995, *Computer Contracts*, with coauthor Richard Morgan; and that same year, along with coauthors Joe Goldblatt and Lisa Delpy, *The Ultimate Guide to Sport Event Management and Marketing*; *Shareholders' Agreements*, with coauthor Janet Jones; *Teens Can Make It Happen: Nine Steps to Success*, in 2000—another edition has a workbook; and, the most recent, as previously mentioned, *Build Your Own Life Brand: A Powerful Strategy to Maximize Your Potential and Enhance Your Value for Ultimate Achievement*, in 2001. Several of the books have appeared in both hardcover and paperback, and at least one with audiotapes.

Whether or not there will ever be a wedding between Stedman Graham and Oprah, the *National Enquirer* often reports on such an event. Writer Jim Nelson, in the May 14, 2002, issue, headlined his two-page story, "Oprah's Surprise Wedding," as if marriage were inevitable, and soon. The inside information, he stated, came from people close to the star. What has brought on this abrupt shift in plans? According to the story, it took the events of September 11, 2001, to convince Oprah of the importance of living in the present.

A further statement Nelson attributed to one of Oprah's friends has to do with the issue of weight and the influence of photos printed by the *National Enquirer* in February 2002. Identifying his informant only as a "source," Nelson writes of a tearful, overweight Oprah's decision that it was time to change—to lose weight and marry; once she announced it to Graham—the story goes on—the two proceeded to make elaborate wedding plans for a small, private wedding on an island. After the private wedding, followed by an equally private 10-day yacht trip, supposedly they would hold a party in Chicago, at Harpo headquarters. The fairy-tale conclusion to this ends with Oprah and Graham's plan for the future.

One week after the publication of Nelson's piece, another Oprah story was published in another tabloid, *The Globe*. Written by reporter Steve Herz, "Oprah's Secret Plan to 'Disappear,' " also is said to come from an Oprah insider.

The journalist reported that he was told that Oprah is "miserable" in the life she leads. None of that was apparent to her devoted following, but he claimed that she wanted to change the way she lived. Her plan for the future apparently was to marry and live with Stedman Graham on the island of Maui. To fulfill that dream, she and her partner, trainer, and friend, Bob Greene, bought property on the Hawaiian island of Maui, where, on a vacation, the story goes, she felt a powerful spiritual connection. That strong force was said to have led her to consider building a large number of structures encompassing not only an Asian-style villa for herself and Graham but also cottages, conference centers, and spas, in a spiritual type of village.

Are any of these stories based on fact? Or are they just another spin on the endless Oprah stories? Only time will tell. Meanwhile, tabloid gossip such as this continues to sell papers. Anything and everything true, exaggerated, rumored, or actually false about Oprah is turned into major news by the tabloids. The statement made years ago in an article by Barbara Grizzuti Harrison that the tabloids make a weekly prediction of the end of the relationship, still holds true. None of the "insider" statements published in the tabloids seems realistic when we read Stedman Graham's books about the strength of their relationship and commitment to each other. By his own declaration, through his personal growth, he has learned to accept Oprah's career with both its fame and difficulties. As for Oprah's feelings about Graham, another observation by Grizzuti Harrison, in "The Importance of Being Oprah," although written several years ago, still seems pertinent. "When she is with Stedman," says Harrison, "her body regains its comfortable eloquence. She vamps." Those tabloids also intersperse stories of the end with stories of an upcoming marriage. No matter the contradictions from issue to issue and from one tabloid to another, the newspaper racks are immediately emptied with each so-called new story. Thus, the cover story, with photo, of the November 19, 2002, issue of *Globe*, proclaimed "At Last! . . . Oprah Heads to the Altar." Once more, a reporter claimed that an anonymous friend of the star provided intimate information about events leading up to Stedman Graham's second proposal in 10 years—the first, which had been reported by several sources, took place in October 1992. The recent proposal, the ring, the acceptance, the engagement party for two were all described in the tabloid, in prose befitting a romance novel. Surprisingly, hardly any information is forthcoming from the so-called friend about the wedding plans, only the statement that Graham wanted a prenuptial agreement and that Gayle King would be the matron of honor. As always, everything in the tabloids remains suspect until, or if ever, Oprah herself goes public with the announcement.

Over the years public interest in Oprah's love life has become a source of humor to her. When she gave the commencement address at Wellesley College in 1997, on the occasion of Wendy Graham's graduation, she joked about her relationship with Wendy's father, identifying him as her "beau," and her "fiancé," but instructing the audience not to ask her when they were going to get married. Nothing has changed since that time, as far as the public knows. More recently, on her April 25, 2003, program, a relaxed and humorous Oprah told stories about herself, once more talking of the astonishing interest in the question of marriage. Poking fun at the inventiveness of the tabloids, she mocked some of the stories printed about her, including the one about Stedman's so-called second proposal in November 2002, "on his knees." And, the story continued, a much moved and responsive woman said "yes."

Amused by all the folderol, a laughing Oprah notifies all who are interested: "If I wanted to be married, I would have been married already."

Chapter 6

BAD FOOD, GOOD FOOD, WEIGHT, AND EXERCISE

A charming story Oprah tells focuses on her love of reading as a small girl. Because she was lonely and isolated when she lived with her grandmother, she had to make do with farm animals for companions, and, inasmuch as her precocity included Bible study, she read Bible stories to the pigs. Whatever affection she might have felt in childhood for the pigs, however, did not affect her eating habits for a number of decades. She ate pork for the next 40 years. According to Howard Lyman's recollection of a private conversation, reported in his book *Mad Cowboy*, it was only after Oprah saw the movie *Babe* that she stopped eating pork. Animated pigs seem to have had a greater influence than live ones on her sensibilities.

Lyman met Oprah on April 16, 1996, when he appeared on her television show to talk about the subject filling many a news broadcast, editorial page, and column: mad cow disease, the vernacular term given to bovine spongiform encephalopathy or Creutzfeld-Jakob disease. Although beef products were not the only item discussed on the show called "Dangerous Foods," it was beef that garnered all the attention. A large number of people in Great Britain were affected by the virulent illness that came from diseased cows. Healthy cows were becoming sick through ingesting the processed meat of infected cattle in their feed. Unknowingly, the practice of providing such food to animals had become common, and only after a significant number of reports of human illness occurred were investigations launched. Important studies had been done, large numbers of farms were isolated, and remedies were being taken. But fear of the possibility of eating contaminated beef spread in Europe. So concerned were citizens throughout the continent that many countries banned the import of British beef.

In the United States, because of reassuring statements issued by various government agencies, few people worried about contracting the illness. Those who planned to vacation abroad simply decided to avoid consumption of beef. However, when Lyman discussed the matter of mad cow disease, he warned the audience that the diet of cows could result in spreading the malady to humans who ate beef. A firestorm arose after Oprah, hearing that thousands of people might contract the illness from eating infected meat, announced that she would no longer eat another burger. If there had been any doubt, anywhere, about her influence, it became clear once the economy was affected: *Business Week* reported a sharp drop in cattle futures after Oprah's show. Several estimates give the figure as 10 percent.

The meat industry reacted furiously to her remarks, highlighting their worry about the effect of the program. When Oprah rejected beef, some people compared her statements to the first President Bush's rejection of broccoli; however, in spite of the irritation and complaints of farmers who raise that vegetable, the president's dislike of broccoli didn't have much of an impact on its general consumption. In contrast to what happened with the broccoli incident, the matter of unsafe beef did not die down. Oprah's audience, largely composed of women who generally do the household shopping, is extremely important to all parts of the food industry, and if those shoppers are told dramatically that a food is unsafe, they will act on the information. Although Lyman found Oprah "gutsy" for dealing with the topic and expressing her personal reaction to the issue, the network lost hundreds of thousands of advertising dollars. When cattle futures fell after her talk show, a group of Texas cattlemen sued both Oprah and Lyman, claiming her presentation had disseminated false and misleading information about U.S. beef that cost them millions of dollars in lost revenue. A gibing report in *Business Week* referred to the group of infuriated ranchers as "boneheads" for bringing suit and expecting Oprah to pay millions for the estimated damage to their business. Oprah herself, at one point, was so discouraged by the events that she talked about settling the case. She was concerned about whether Americans would be inclined to feel sympathy for the beef industry or whether their substantial affection for her would place them on her side. Powerful though the beef lobby is, those who followed the case believed in Oprah's civic mindedness, whereas her lawyers based major arguments on the constitutional provision of free speech.

A plaintiff's attorney pointed out that the television program emanated from Chicago, suggesting its difference from the South and identifying one of the underlying antagonisms of the lawsuit. There was also an undercurrent of the color issue. Oprah herself, half-jokingly, half-seriously, referred to herself as "Black coming" when she first arrived in the area. With her always-open attitude about color, in any region Oprah's world is all encompassing. Oprah's presence in Texas, in confronting those suing her, confirms her proud father's statements to interviewers: that his daughter is not simply a good role model for any single group, but for everyone. Her strength, dignity, and determination to carry on her television program reinforce her father's views.

A number of cattlemen, uninvolved in the lawsuit, voiced concern about beef in America, and the effect of mixing imported beef with home-grown beef. These ranchers wanted foreign beef to be inspected and labeled. However, Lyman and Oprah did not focus on that issue. Lyman, as a vegetarian, did not differentiate one beef product from another, and without grandstanding, Oprah simply announced her decision to give up "burgers."

Although the television program was aired in 1996, the case did not come to court until 1998; the plaintiffs expected it would be the first test of a 1995 Texas so-called veggie law, protecting perishable foods. They had every reason to expect the ruling to be favorable to them; in addition to Texas, more than a dozen other states throughout the country had passed legislation against what was called food defamation, to protect farmers and ranchers against various types of consumer groups. However, U.S. District Judge Mary Lou Robinson ruled against their complaint, because she said that the law was not applicable to "hoofed products." The request of Oprah's attorneys to have the case dismissed was also denied when, after four weeks of testimony, the plaintiffs rested their case. Oprah's lawyers put on a show-and-tell performance of their own with pictures of bloody, cut-up animal parts used in making feed for live cattle. When she was called to the stand, her own testimony had two major points; the first held that as a talk show host she is not required to have the objectivity of a news reporter; the second point focused on her efforts to offer balanced coverage of the issues, by inviting pro- as well as anti-beef guests to present their views. In fact, initially the beef industry had not been concerned about the planned appearance of Howard Lyman, seeing him both as an antimeat crusader and a vegetarian activist. Clearly, the trade association underestimated the Oprah effect and the size of her audience.

Oprah shifted her entire show to Amarillo so that she could continue with her program for the duration of the trial. In what was described in an editorial in the *Washington Post* as a "circus-like" atmosphere, the trial took place. With the heated circumstances and surroundings, even unfortunately chosen terms used by a witness took on a novelistic character. In his testimony, a Maryland professor, William Hueston, spoke of the "lynch mob" thinking revealed on the program, language for which he later apologized emotionally, explaining he'd meant no racial offense. Hueston, a former U.S. Department of Agriculture spokesman, had been on the original show and was not considered friendly afterward. He complained that he had not been treated well and had been given only a brief time to present his probeef argument. On the stand, however, he was both contrite and tearful.

In a case that normally would have caused little stir, every step of this trial made news. Experts and nonexperts were quoted in the press. Not only did newspeople follow and report frequently on the events, but townspeople saw the trial as a major event. In spite of the admonitions of the president of the Chamber of Commerce about any unusual display of welcome to the star, the people of Amarillo regarded her presence as a singular and exciting event. Lines formed daily at the courthouse, and fans were everywhere, inside and outside the courtroom. Newspapers and magazines were filled with pictures and stories of the comings and goings of the actors. Generally people in the area sided with Oprah, but a handful were rude and hostile, such as those who displayed bumper stickers claiming that the only mad cow to be concerned with was Oprah. Nevertheless, a group with opposing views proclaimed vigorously, "We love you, Oprah."

Those closest to Oprah personally took turns providing her with support: Stedman Graham, Gayle King, and Maya Angelou. They said that they wanted to show love and solidarity through their presence. Angelou sent a group of preachers to Texas to pray for Oprah on a daily basis. Oprah kept going, putting on her daily television show in spite of all the turmoil, showing the strength that led to her success. As Gayle King points out, Oprah is no whiner and dislikes those who are.

In the end, the jury of eight women and four men found the defendants not guilty of the charge. But that wasn't the conclusion of the matter. The ranchers took the case to the fifth U.S. Circuit Court of Appeals, which, two years later, upheld the lower court's verdict. The court of appeals called the show's presentation melodramatic, yet ruled that the information given on the program was neither false nor defamatory. David J. Bederman, a professor at Emory University pointed to the irony of the victory when he stated in newspaper articles that Oprah had won in spite of the fact that the cattlemen had been able to choose both locale and jury for the trial. His judgment was reinforced in later reports by multiple newspapers and magazines. Typical of some views was that of *Time* magazine, which noted rather dramatically that Oprah was more powerful than the law.

The case was over, but in spite of the changes required by the British government and put in place by the British cattle industry, the people continued to question the safety of British beef. Exposés appeared about the culture of beef and the dangers of the slaughterhouse to workers, including illness and maiming. Nevertheless, burgers, which defenders of the American way compare to the importance of apple pie, still are the major item for fast food restaurants; steak houses, which often serve hamburgers as well as steak, continue to flourish and actually have become more numerous throughout the country. Oprah does not discuss beef on her show or in her magazine anymore.

Chicken as a favorite food now is king, although that industry has been and continues to be the subject of many an exposé in newspapers, magazines, and documentaries. The unsanitary condition of poultry processing plants, the effect of slaughter and runoffs into water areas, and above all the frequent warnings about bacterial infection are reported constantly. However, television talk shows, including Oprah's, have not taken on the poultry industry even though there have been numerous exposés, far more than those of the beef industry.

Food is a frequent topic for Oprah. She has said that she likes chicken. Recipes for poultry dishes appear in her magazine and in cookbooks she touts; she has spoken of chicken breasts, marinated and broiled or baked, as one of her favorite foods. She has also said that another favorite food is potatoes—cooked in any form known to chefs. All Oprah watchers know she has had a chef for years, and often she has declared she has no knowledge of cooking, yet, in one of her revelations about dieting and its difficulties, she talked of broiling chicken breasts for Stedman's dinner during one of her periods of food deprivation. This was at a time when she declared that her diet resolution was so strong that she watched him eat the chicken while she ate a low-calorie, healthier meal.

Oprah's audience knows many almost-intimate details about her battle with weight and control of eating. Such issues have been the subject of numerous shows, confessions, and interviews. Even movie reviewers work in comments about these matters, as in a column by Rebecca Dana describing the film *Under the Tuscan Sun*: the writer watching the picture is reminded of conversations "among girlfriends over tea at a Barnes & Noble café. Which is to say, it is obsessed with food and eating in an Oprah audience kind of way."

The entire viewing world seems to watch the struggle that has provided endless material for the press—particularly but not only the tabloids—to dine on. Stories about Oprah's weight, or any of her other activities, sell newspapers, not only the popular ones but also those whose entire existence depends on various tidbits of gossip about well-known people.

Uncomplimentary remarks and unattractive photos often appear in the tabloids, but other newspapers and magazines were not kind to Oprah in earlier years, either. Unflattering photos accompanied by narration often dwelt on her weight problems, even though such pictures seem a strange contrast to the healthy, fit displays of Oprah in her own magazine over the same general time period. Yet Oprah herself has made the subject of her weight a very public topic on television, in interviews, and in her magazine.

A tabloid piece, published in 2001, quoted a so-called friend or a source, speaking on Oprah's terror about her health, that is, the effect of her weight on her physical well-being; the "friend" was quoted as saying the star has "early signs of heart disease," that she could have a heart attack or a stroke. Yet, on several television shows following the issue of that story, Oprah spoke of her good health and referred to numerous physical tests she had taken. However, in O, she spoke of her health concerns when she developed unexplained physical symptoms. Was she responding obliquely to the story in the tabloid? She has often declared her scorn for such papers. Nevertheless, hurtful as they are, she has also been known to read things written about her, although she declared publicly in the last few years that she no longer pays attention to tabloids. And, even if one wanted to avoid the tabloids, it is almost impossible—they are everywhere. So, in her programs about emotional eating and menopause, she spoke humorously of some signs and symptoms that had worried her but ultimately had nothing to do with her health. As with other women of her age, they were a prelude to menopause, a physical change she had denied—she says laughingly to her friend and trainer Bob Greene, who had broached the subject with her and later appeared March 15, 2002, on her program about "Emotional Eating." It turned out that the story in the paper actually had some elements of truth; but by the time the piece was printed, it was old and discarded news. Yes, Oprah told her audience and readers that she had been worried by heart palpitations, but she was informed by doctor after doctor, five in all, that she had no heart problems. However, none of the physicians could diagnose the cause of her symptoms. Even after mentioning her concern to Bob Greene while running with him, she rejected his suggestion that it might be what everyone has been calling "the big M." It was her accidental discovery of a book, *The Wisdom of Menopause*, that she recognized the problem described and explained. In reading the chapter "Palpitations: Your Heart's Wake-Up Call," she identified what was happening to her.

And yet, the tabloids are relentless in their pursuit. Their reporters appear to go everywhere she does. Photographers take pictures at every opportunity. When fresh information or readership appears to be flagging in the tabloids, a familiar refrain is sounded, that Oprah is "out of control," and her poundage is deadly. Photos one month of a fat, unappealing, even ugly woman may precede or follow those of a stunning-looking Oprah, such as the time she was shown in a black silk ruffled dress—also appearing in an issue of her magazine.

Tabloid photos of September 10, 2002, become questionable when compared with Oprah's appearance only 12 days later for the fifty-fourth annual Emmy Awards. The ceremony was televised live, thus preventing any possibility of alteration. While not thin, Oprah was praised by a number of fashion critics as being svelte and stunning in a white silk gown. That same shot of Oprah in the white gown appeared in October, along with pictures of other entertainers, on the cover of *People* magazine, making the point that women of all sizes can be sexy. Furthermore, in its end-of-year 2002 issue, that same magazine ran the article "Dresses of the Year," again showing Oprah in her gorgeous Bradley Bayou white silk garment.

Someone designated by the sensationalist paper, the *National Enquirer*, in its September 10, 2002, edition as a "pal," and another as an "inside" source are said to have provided information about a vacationing Oprah. He/she/they are credited with descriptions of their "friend" in the most unfriendly and unattractive language possible: "swollen" and "puffy," with rippled flesh of "peaks and valleys." These sources, always unnamed and outspoken, tell of a current lifestyle, a pattern of uncontrolled eating and minimal exercise. The guilty food enumerated by her "pal" belongs to the typically favorite American choices of chips, fried chicken, and high-calorie desserts, all the things that Oprah once confessed to craving. But on many occasions she also has told her audience and readers that she no longer indulges in her old food habits.

Discussions of eating and weight may be the most frequently aired top-ics of her show. They are also the subject of interviews she has given. Even white South Africans, in a country where racial issues remain a major problem, have voiced more interest in her weight than in her race. View-ers often take a cue from Oprah's preoccupations, reflecting them. For Oprah and many others, food has been more than a necessity for exis-tence. Her frequently voiced message stresses that food may be all out of proportion to physical need, that it fills an emotional void. Oprah points out that food for her has served as substitution for love and that it can briefly replace the deficiency of affection. In her deprived youth, when she was friendless, neglected, and sexually abused, food represented the secu-rity she always needed and wanted. She compares food addiction to alco-hol and drug addition, seeing the basic causes for all three as the same. Psychologists would say that the physicality of food resembles the emo-tional need narcissistic personalities require through constant assurances of admiration, attention, and concern from those around them. Just as the narcissistic person can never be "filled" because of the emptiness within, so too the food addict. Not surprisingly, similar to the never-ending ob-sessive and compulsive requirements of the narcissist, food momentarily masks insecurity, loneliness, anger, pain, and even despair.

Does Oprah comfort herself with food when there are problems or ten-sion or worries? She would be the first to acknowledge that happened in the past; but she also has said for some time that she understands the is-sues and is now able to deal with the matter of food as an emotional crutch. She declares that she has learned over the years that many of the hidden problems she once denied were blocked by food.

Confident and persistent though she has been in her growing aware-ness of the sources of her emotional approach to food, Oprah had the same struggle at times with food as an alcoholic with liquor. Stress, over-work, and worry cause her to overeat. In talking about the tension she felt during the court hearings in Texas, she points to the exhaustion that came from the dual activities of being in court for entire days and keeping her television show going: with her level of resistance to comfort foods at a low, she gave in to the temptations of sweets, eating forbidden desserts such as pie. The result, in a rather brief period of time, was a weight gain of 11 pounds.

The yo-yo syndrome has been a large part of Oprah's adult life. When her movie *Beloved* opened, Oprah was invited to appear on the cover of *Vogue*, the magazine of fashion, glamour, and beauty. But the editors re-quired that Oprah lose 20 pounds before being photographed. Underscoring the importance of the film for her, she endured a formidable program that combined dieting and workouts with her personal trainer, Bob Greene. Oprah claims nobody her size ever before appeared on the cover of *Vogue*, and extends that to women past 30, as well as black women. She lost the required weight for the *Vogue* shoot but confessed that she'd lost the same amount of weight before filming *Beloved* and then had put it on again. In fact, she had lost weight only a few years earlier for the September 1995 cover of *Redbook*. Oprah's picture was said to boost sales of that magazine to the highest of the year. It is obvious that a picture of Oprah on a magazine is a selling point even when there is no story at all about her.

Not everyone agrees with Oprah's decision to conform to the requirements of *Vogue*'s editors. Writing for *World Book Online*, Marilyn Gardner questions the entire idea of the star's having a makeover, of being placed in the category of a supermodel just to sell a magazine or publicize a movie. After all, Oprah's fans, Gardner, and countless other writers find her lovely even without the transformation. Without taking away any kudos from Oprah's tenaciousness in weight loss, people admire Oprah no matter her dress size. The issue raised by Gardner is one that Oprah herself has touched on, warily to be sure—given her own somewhat obsessive search for the holy grail of the body beautiful. Isn't the message that slenderness is all that matters harmful and destructive, particularly in our culture where anorexia and bulimia take a terrible toll in the lives of young women?

Oprah's weight has gone up and down with frequency. Once, at a boxing match, she made the unhappy discovery that at 216 pounds she weighed the same as heavyweight fighter Mike Tyson. When she was awarded a trophy at the Emmy Awards in 1987, she was up to 226 pounds. And that was not her highest weight. During the period of her transition from Baltimore to Chicago, she had weighed 238 pounds; however, that did not interfere with her debut in a new program, nor her recognition that nobody like her had ever been on television. Over the years her weight has varied as much as 100 pounds.

Since her early working days she has been a number of different sizes, a fact that still distresses her; yet in a poll taken by *People* magazine about the question of weight and image, Oprah was the favorite of all age groups as the most helpful person for the image of larger women. Many women like the fact that Oprah is their size. Putting a spin on some of that approval, Oprah psychologized that her overweight condition helped keep viewers from becoming jealous. Women may resent her success, her wealth, her lifestyle—homes, cars, clothes, and a handsome lover, but, she hypothesizes, they can handle that by finding her flaw, her Achilles' heel, the imperfection in her weight.

During one of her slim periods, when she dropped from a "women's" size 22 to a "misses" size 8—temporarily—she contributed 900 dresses to a charity auction. The auction was a great success, not only because these were celebrity garments but also because some of the clothing still had their original tags, and some were auctioned for a third of their purchase price. Even at her most attractive, Oprah can never be a small woman; with a size 10 shoe size, a height of five foot six, and a large frame, she really was not meant to be a size 8, even though she has struggled constantly to achieve it. Always so concerned about her weight, she has rejected the fact that fans and admirers see her as glamorous at any weight and are indifferent to her size. Reporters, however, are often critical. Looking for eye-catching language or sound bites, they have described her as, for example, "zaftig" (well-endowed). One year a television magazine published on its cover a cobbled-together photo of her—beautiful but fake—Oprah's head and Ann-Margret's body, a portrait that both stars found insulting. Although the avowed intention of the weekly was to underscore the fact of Oprah's dominant financial position in television, the story backfired when the fakery was exposed.

When interviewers have commented on the fact that Oprah has always been outspoken about her weight, she responds by saying that she never tried to be anyone other than herself; further, she believes that we have an obsession with weight in the United States. Nobody would argue with that view, but it does not appear to have diminished Oprah's own personal preoccupation with size, which she speaks about more often than any other problem in her adult life. Addiction to Oprah spells food, and one of her special 10 commandments, number six, requires the forswearing of addiction of any kind. Although in the past Oprah drank and took drugs, those days are long behind her, but she constantly fights her addiction to food.

While saying that she needs only to be herself, Oprah seems to believe in a quote appearing on a poster in her Chicago home, a saying of the good witch Glinda, from the *Wizard of Oz*, "You don't need to be helped any longer." Although the witch assures the young girl, Dorothy, that she "always had the power," and Oprah espouses that view, she always needed help from various sources. In her search for support, she tells her audience and interviewers, she tried every diet advertised, and some of them worked—briefly. In 1989, with a goal of fitting into a size 10 dress, Oprah lost 67 pounds on an Optifast liquid diet, to weigh in at 142. To show her television audience what that much poundage looked like, she pulled across the stage a slab of fat the equivalent of the weight she'd lost. Two years earlier she had turned to a nutritionist for help in losing weight; she weighed 180, and she managed to lose 20 pounds. Although she lost this weight, by jogging and dieting, the loss did not occur fast enough to suit her. That was when she decided to go on a physician-supervised Optifast liquid diet, in addition to exercising and working with her cook.

Soon after Oprah reached her goal of 142, she regained 17 pounds, and with that came the recognition there was no quick fix for weight problems. Coincidentally, at about that same time she became a partner with Richard Melman in a Chicago restaurant called the Eccentric. For Melman, who is a friend of Oprah's and boyfriend Stedman Graham's, this was the fourth dining establishment in which he was involved. Although all four places are in the city, his business group has restaurants in different states as well as abroad. A large restaurant, the Eccentric was built in a remodeled warehouse. The restaurant featured different types of cuisines and bars, from small and intimate rooms and meals to larger dining areas, as well as a busy, noisy disco: something for everyone, even in choices of foods of various cultures. The menu's offerings ran the gamut from light and health-conscious items to the fare one would expect in a city famous for its beef, with prices beginning in the moderate range and going upward.

Oprah was interested in being part of a restaurant not only because she was fixated on food for most of her life, but also because she wanted to have a special place to go, to entertain and bring friends, to be able to dance and to eat food she enjoys. Even her espoused love of potatoes found its way onto the menu, with her "signature dish," which isn't secret at all: the recipe appears in her magazine, a recipe for rather lumpy potatoes mashed with horseradish and cream. Since Oprah followers all know about her love of potatoes—she makes frequent, exclamatory statements about that food—it isn't surprising that the specialty ones were extremely popular among people first visiting the Eccentric. Perhaps, for someone with a weight problem, owning and enjoying frequent visits to her restaurant appear to be another way of undermining her resolve to control her weight. That and her avowed, often uncontrollable indulgence in junk food and sweet desserts have defeated her best intentions periodically.

In 1991 Oprah decided to try another tack in the ongoing saga of weight control. As she told her television audience, her change in strategy came after she'd been following one diet or another for many years.

She'd gone from shopping in boutiques for the slender figure to the next size and finally to those for the larger woman. Even though she'd had a trainer/cook combination for a while, her weight fluctuated as she lost and regained pounds. After she and Graham took a luxury cruise on the Mediterranean, she was dismayed once again by her weight gain, then up to 205 pounds.

At Cal-a-Vie spa, a southern California weight-reduction spa, where Oprah took a health-focused vacation, she met the chef, Rosie Daley, who, like Stedman Graham, came from New Jersey. Unlike him, however, she is part of a large Irish-American family of 13 children, and, unlike Oprah, Rosie is a small and petite woman. Even though she didn't plan to be a cook, she'd been doing kitchen work in her family from the age of six onward; in adulthood, when she moved to California, she discovered she could support herself by working in restaurants, going from the role of assistant to cooks to becoming a full-fledged chef on her own. Oprah, finding that a week did not make a great impact on her size, felt she had to find a different and longer route toward weight control. Impressed by the quality of Daley's cooking and the health advantage offered in making low-calorie food taste delicious, Oprah offered Daley a job as her personal chef, "begged" her, according to Oprah. It took six months of persuasion for Rosie to accept. Reluctant at first, Daley did not want to uproot herself and her son—she liked her job and had rejected overtures from other people; also, she is a single parent who found California a good place to raise a child. But Oprah made a financial offer she couldn't refuse. Although the monetary arrangement was not made public, it was touted as being liberal, in keeping with the demands of Oprah's somewhat peripatetic lifestyle. As the owner of several homes, Oprah travels between them, from one to another—Chicago, Indiana, California, Colorado, and previously, Florida. Rosie, did not live with Oprah but prepared all the Chicago meals in the high-rise lakeside condo: first thing in the morning she readied lunch and nibbles, which she would take to the studio; later she would return to the apartment to make dinner for Oprah and Stedman; and, her last chore of the evening would be leaving a small but healthful breakfast of juice and muffins. One perk of Rosie's job was that someone else took care of any washing-up duties.

Rosie, who always had an interest in art but failed to become an artist, transferred her inclination toward design to the aesthetic presentations of food. She has said, written, and demonstrated that appearance of a meal is very important to consumption and enjoyment. After becoming a part of Oprah's life for several years, in spite of several lapses on Oprah's part,

Rosie succeeded much of the time in changing her food habits from fried and starchy to vegetables, fruits, salads, and grains. In her book, *In the Kitchen with Rosie*, which she wrote after becoming Oprah's chef, she tells the reader she chose recipes that are Oprah's own "all-time favorites."

Oprah reminisces in Rosie's book about the enormous, mouth-watering "daily feasts," the weekday and Sunday dinners her Grandmother Lee would prepare. The foods of her childhood were those of most Southern families, and still are for many. Breakfast meant "cheese grits" with "homemade biscuits" that were "smothered in butter," along with the ever-present, essential accompaniment of southern "red-eyed gravy" and "home-cured ham." Humorously, Oprah emphasizes that kind of meal was "just breakfast." Dinner, during the week, was yet more caloric, with offerings of chicken that was "smothered" or fried, along with vegetables raised on the farm, like "butter beans," or foods that could be made from home-grown corn, such as corn bread. Even though the Lees were poor, food was plentiful, and for Oprah it represented all the things a lonely, almost parentless child longed for: "security and comfort.... love." Naturally, like all children, she did not think about healthful versus unhealthful food; she didn't have to, and even if she did, in the simple world in which she spent her early childhood there would have been no opportunity to change the diet. The family ate what it could grow or raise, and that was that.

Rosie established certain rules about eating healthful foods and holding certain attitudes about food. The most important issue seems to be consciousness of the composition of foods, that is, finding foods that avoid fat and are not high in calories. These tricks are familiar to anyone who has been on a diet. There is no magic, but there are some useful and tasteful food substitutes.

Happily for Oprah, she began to see results from the change of diet, plus another alteration in her style of living—regular exercise. But for someone growing up as she did, the early, fixed food patterns do not disappear completely. Since food always has served as her source of comfort, her solace when events do not turn out as well as she wanted, she hasn't invariably followed Daley's instructions. Under stress, her typical response has been binge eating.

Oprah declares that she's read every diet book ever published, including those of Geneen Roth, which emphasize the emotional aspect of overeating. Roth's books, Oprah claims, helped her to understand it isn't physical need that sets appetite in motion but a refusal to face up to emotional problems. Like most overweight people, Oprah wanted a miracu-

lous cure, even though she knows the so-called whys and wherefores of
binging and dieting and the role that food plays when one wants to avoid
or ignore the problems that lead to addiction.

Oprah's weight problems are so familiar to millions—sometimes it
seems like the entire planet—her name gets bandied about whenever any
news columnist writes about someone who has even the most remote similarity to any of Oprah's problems. One instance appears in a food column
from the *New York Times*. More than a page and a half are given over to
the work of a British cook named Nigella Lawson, star of a cooking show
in Britain, *Nigella Bites*, which also is on E! Entertainment Television and
the Style network in the United States. Lawson has written two cookbooks: *How to Eat* and *How to Be a Domestic Goddess*. The connection
with Oprah is extremely tenuous, but the stretch is made by *New York
Times* food writer and columnist Amanda Hesser. Where Lawson was described in an issue of *Gourmet* as resembling a film star, critic Hesser dis-
agrees. Hesser says that she finds Lawson more like the mythical everyman
(or everywoman), with ordinary problems much like the rest of the public. Writing of Lawson's family, job, and battles with weight, Hesser refers
to "the Oprah Winfrey effect." The thrust of that is no matter how exciting a life a star leads, how more glamorous and different as it may seem
from that of the average housewife, close examination reveals the same
troubles of other working women; therefore the reader/audience "can
trust her every word." Hesser's point seems a reflection and even a repeti-
tion of the remarks Oprah herself has made. Others can "forgive" a star
who only *seems* to have everything. But in reality, Oprah—and Lawson—
do have their own Achilles' heel. Nonetheless, Lawson's struggles with
weight do not appear to be as extreme or destructive as Oprah's; still, according to Adrienne Ressler, identified as a "body image specialist," in a
survey taken by *People* in September 2000, the queen of daytime television stands above the question of weight or body image.

In fact, even if the star herself doesn't accept it, over the years many
journalists have referred to her as fabulous, unforgettable, and one of the
most beautiful women in the world. If she follows a particular diet plan,
magazines and newspapers seize on it, publish it and sell papers; undoubtedly, the diet industry has also been able to benefit from any tie-in that
could be made (as with Optifast) between a product and Oprah. Star
power sells diets. In a similar case, England's Sarah Ferguson, the Duchess
of York, known as "Fergie," has been a drawing card for Weight Watchers.
Women's magazines, in particular, will feature articles about one diet plan
or another, as they come and go, about the efficacy of a particular program

for a famous person, thus making the connection to the reading public. A reporter wrote that yoga classes everywhere filled after an appearance by Madonna on one of Oprah's shows, when she mentioned that she was practicing yoga. Nevertheless, as *Consumer Reports* states in a June 2002 feature, "The Truth About Dieting," many Americans think they cannot lose weight unless they lead the privileged life of someone like Oprah, with both a personal chef and trainer. Even Oprah's own magazine shows gorgeous and/or famous people who have improved their health, with fantastic results. The magazine does not feature the failures.

It is not remarkable, then, that Rosie Daley's book, *In the Kitchen with Rosie*, became a smash hit almost immediately on publication. Called the fastest-selling book in American publishing, it is reputed to have sold 6 million copies. Published in 1995 by Alfred Knopf, its success had to be attributable in large measure to the Oprah connection. A demonstration show, "Oprah and Rosie's Cooking School," put on by the two women in 1993 was also well-received. In her statements in the book Oprah gives high praise to the recipes. Oprah frequently reiterates her rules about the importance of controlling food, diet, and exercise: she follows Rosie's belief that healthful food can be pleasurable to eat and that anyone may easily find substitutes for items that are not acceptable. Further, after Oprah met Bob Greene, the person who became her guide to exercise, and she'd read the recommendations of Dr. Dean Ornish, she also began to advocate sensible forms of exercise, which, for most people is a daily walk.

Three years earlier, Oprah had selected Knopf as the publisher of her proposed autobiography, a book ballyhooed from the moment the announcement was made that she'd be writing her life story. The publisher expected the book to be a huge seller, given the size of Oprah's audience. However, even after the almost complete manuscript was readied by a ghostwriter, Oprah withdrew from the contract, determined her autobiography would not be published, at least in the foreseeable future. Thus, the Rosie Daley book provided consolation for Knopf, because of its immediate success. The book was so popular that after a time Rosie was able to give up cooking for a living.

Without Oprah, Daley's book would have been only another health-conscious, eat-well recipe book. But cooking for Oprah made Daley rich, both in wages as chef and in sales of a book rather small in size and scope, in effect a book about the star's dinners at home—when she is at home. Combined with the suggestion that the reader also can prepare the same meals Oprah eats and lose weight like Oprah, the book provides cachet that could hardly lose.

For Daley's text, Oprah wrote an introduction; her name is on the cover; there are attractive pictures and Oprah remarks scattered throughout. The book is dedicated to "Oprah and Stedman," described by Rosie as "wonderful" to work for, and she adds the requisite "thank you" for all that she was permitted to do as their chef. Naturally, given the spa cooking background of Daley, the emphasis in her beginning remarks as well as throughout the work is on healthful food. Each and every recipe is regarded as a creation, both beautiful to look at and good for the body. The food is so sin-free that one would have to eat very large amounts to put on any weight at all.

This is no Julia Child's cookbook, which has numerous rich, French-style recipes. Oprah has said that she doesn't care much for French food, and that seems apparent in Daley's book. Her tastes run more to spices and island type of cooking. For Daley, verboten foods are those ingredients at the heart of French cooking: butter, whole milk, cream, and oils. Also disallowed are "real" fried items, the heart and soul of country cooking. But Rosie and Oprah use an important substitute technique called "unfrying." The "un-fried" foods now become a different kind of potatoes, crab cakes, catfish, and chicken, what Rosie, and presumably Oprah, find delicious substitutes for the old-fashioned, deep-fried familiar dishes of a Southern childhood.

The book is basic, as if intended for an inexperienced, beginning cook with simple directions for kitchen organization, shopping for and preparation of food, creating visual appeal, and substituting not only healthful but low-calorie ingredients. The recipes provide details of many easy meals. The first item covered is soup, the food Oprah consumes on a daily basis, and with Oprah's brief description of her love of soup, the format of the book is established. Each segment includes a few sentences from Oprah in which she tells the reader that soup and a sandwich are lunch choices in winter, changing to soup and salad in summer. Along with directions for shopping and preparation, Daley lists ingredients, fat grams and calories, and number of servings. The soups differ from the average recipe described in traditional cookbooks, in that they contain many herbs and spices, some of which have to be bought in specialty or mail-order stores.

Inasmuch as the book is intended to be an intimate look at what this particular star eats, the chapters designate food for Oprah's specific palate. Daley does not repudiate the popular—and fattening—forms of pasta, pizza, and topping recipes found in restaurants or grocery stores—she just alters them. After all, Americans have been eating these foods for a long period of time, and Oprah writes in the short introduction to this segment that she has pasta five times a week, and names the varieties of pasta. She and Rosie both seem to like the idea of mixing various kinds of dough and sauces. Oprah never speaks of getting bored by her diet. But it is difficult to believe that someone leading Oprah's glamorous life would be able to restrict herself to five nights a week of pasta. Oprah, like many people, also enjoys pizza. Even though few would consider pizza something a conscientious weight watcher would eat, Rosie explains why her version is all right. The same holds true for her special sauces. Oprah is fond of many different types of sauces, and Daley notes that endless possibilities exist.

Rosie's pesto seems unique: there is none of the usual olive oil in it. Instead, Rosie makes her pesto with lemon juice. Even bruschetta is permissible, a dish usually considered sinfully fattening, but Rosie offers a healthful version. At the end of the pasta chapter, Rosie finishes the segment with a recipe no health-conscious reader or dieter could criticize: grilled vegetable sandwiches. Oprah's southern background becomes obvious again in some of Rosie's vegetable selections, which Oprah finds wonderful. It seems as if the entire world knows of her love for potatoes, so two choices are listed, not the fried kind from childhood days but those that take into account her pleasure in spice. Thus, Roasted Mustard Potatoes are on the menu, as well as another mustard dish, Yogurt Mustard served with Artichokes. There's also a recipe for Potato Gratin, though it isn't the familiar, fattening version.

Could one be a committed dieter without salads? As a southern girl to whom food meant, fry, fry, fry, Oprah grew up disliking salads. Her reason, she states in Rosie's book, was that she considered salads boring. But with her new mode of eating, she changed her mind. What it took was change from iceberg lettuce to varieties she didn't know of. A salad in the South in the days of Oprah's youth, and even later, was something to be tolerated, not enjoyed, a nondescript dish that was always the same from one kitchen or restaurant to another. And, salad dressings were even more pedestrian. While avoiding high-calorie dressings such as the popular Caesar, Rosie introduces beautiful raw vegetables as salads or as interesting foods that could be grilled on the top of the stove. Now, Oprah claims, she likes salads.

With the advent of Rosie in the kitchen, Oprah became a strong advocate of more nourishing foods for everyone. Always having enjoyed inviting company for dinner, once Rosie became her chef, she delighted in serving friends foods that are good for them; she obviously finds that fun, because, she tells the reader, she didn't let on how healthful the menus have been. In the "Entrees" chapter, a low-calorie, low-fat Spanish dish, Paella, was chosen for inclusion because Oprah says that her dinner guests seem particularly fond of it. Also Spanish, but with the American alterations of the Tex-Mex school, is Red Beans and Rice with Salsa, a somewhat spicier presentation of a dish most dieters recognize. Although cost is seldom mentioned in the book, this recipe is easy on both the pocketbook and calories.

Typically, throughout the cookbook, most of the recipes have unusual seasonings, or depart from what a reader expects when the name of the dish is listed. For example, the entree "Roasted Duck with Pineapple Chutney" may seem familiar, but it takes on a wholly different form when Rosie selects the duck. Following her pattern of providing special advice or information about a recipe, here Rosie notes that her version of this particular dish of duck is both elegant and easy. An insert recommends the purchase of a somewhat expensive and hard-to-find Muscovy duck breast, which Rosie recommends because it is both "firm" and "boneless." At the end of the book, the author provides addresses and phone numbers of stores that carry unusual food items. An insert that calls for the purchase of a somewhat expensive and hard-to-find Muscovy duck breast, which Rosie recommends, reminds the reader of Rosie's experience as a cook at spas, where cost is not a matter of concern.

Similar to the end of most meals, the conclusion of the book is about dessert, because Oprah wants something sweet when the meal is finished. If any reader needs reminding that this is spa, healthful, diet food, the titles of the recipes take care of that: "Mango Parfait," "Chocolate Tofu Cake," or "Spiced Bran Muffins." And, if one longs for toppings, there is always "Mock Whipped Cream."

The next person in the kitchen, succeeding Rosie, was Art Smith, formerly chef for numerous celebrities, including Martha Stewart, famous for her household virtues. Unlike the noncook Oprah, Stewart is a woman whose magazine contains her own recipes, whereas Oprah's only food contribution to O seems to be the recipe for her special potatoes. Smith, as working chef for Oprah since 1997, has the featured Christmas menu in the year-end 2002 issue of O. Like Rosie Daley, he is also the author of a cookbook, albeit less well-known, perhaps because Smith doesn't tell readers which meals are Oprah's favorites. However, the introductory heading for the review of Smith's book, in such newspapers as the *Palm Beach Post*, invokes the name of the star: "Oprah's Chef Puts Family Time on Menu." Furthermore, the jacket blurbs of the book, front and back, ensure that the public knows Smith is personal chef to Oprah.

The focus of *Back to the Table: The Reunion of Food and Family*, Smith's cookbook, is very different from Rosie's, although several of his recipes, like Rosie's, contain spices that Oprah favors. He also lists ingredients such as plantains, pumpkin seeds, and Madras curry, items found primarily in Latino markets.

Rosie is businesslike; Art Smith is not. Whereas Rosie is a former New Yorker and Californian, Smith is a southerner, having spent his boyhood in a rural part of Florida, Jasper, in the Panhandle region. Not surprisingly, the foods in his Grandmother Georgia's home resembled those of Oprah's grandmother. Although much of the food was similar in both homes, the houses themselves were different. Grandmother Hattie Mae lived in a tiny wooden house with no running water or indoor plumbing, but Grandmother Georgia's home was a large old Victorian building made of brick, a house where she once had taken in boarders, for whom she provided meals. Smith's grandmother was famous for her biscuits, homemade jams and jellies, and much like Grandmother Lee she served farm-raised vegetables and meats. Southern cooking, whether prepared by black or white people, has always been similar.

Smith's cookbook, undoubtedly reflecting the author himself, is friendly and chatty, filled with little stories and personal reminiscences. He talks of Sunday dinners, church, and "the Lord's day." He philosophizes and advises, using the words "comfort" and "love" again and again, almost interchangeably. "Comfort" includes many meanings and variables; to Smith, food is a symbol of love, whereas for Oprah it has been a substitute for love. For Smith food signifies family, tradition, and renewal. Sharing a meal, he believes, is a celebration of love. For Oprah food has been a shield against the disappointments of life. Where Smith considers food healing, she craved it like a drug, so that all too often it became a destructive agent.

Food cooked with love, according to Smith, undoubtedly provides the catalyst for healing. The *Post* reviewer regarded that view as primary because her second headline for the story about Smith stated, in bold letters: "Advice from Oprah's chef: don't forget to add love." A cynic might consider the idea a sales gimmick, but Smith names his mother, two grandmothers, and an aunt as those who first taught him about food made and served with love. Is that merely sentimental or does it also have the ring of truth, telling the reader that people who love both cooking and serving food to their families have added dimensions in their lives.

Healing and family go together in Smith's view. One aunt's idea of cures for whatever ails a person, is cake, so she sends one to her nephew whenever she thinks he needs solace. That concern for him reflects his years of growing up in a family that spent much time together: they still do. Oprah's family was always split, and even now she may fail to find comfort and love in what remains of her own relatives, but there is strong appeal in Smith's philosophy.

Where Smith thinks the "best" food is related to love, Rosie speaks of food cooked with an eye toward control of calories and fat. A dieting Oprah concerns herself with such things, but memories of the loneliness, lovelessness drew her to Smith's kind of comforting food. Smith's fried chicken reminded her of the food of her childhood, a fond memory of plenitude and warmth in a household ruled by her otherwise harsh and strict grandmother.

Oprah had tried almost desperately to lose weight through diet after diet for years, and even after hiring Rosie as special chef, she learned she had to do more; she found it necessary to add the component of vigorous exercise to succeed. Although she had not been a fat adolescent, from the age of 22, when she first went to work as a coanchor for WJZ-TV in Baltimore, weight became a major issue in her life. Food was more than solace—it was a lifeline. At that time she was renting a home in the suburbs of Maryland, in a planned city called Columbia, where the attractions of the food courts of a nearby mall magnified her problems. In a new job, in a strange town, she began to substitute food for all that was missing in her life. Soon the cycle began that years later led her to Bob Greene, the man who would become her personal trainer, good friend, and longtime assistant. Advertisements for his books describe his expertise in "fitness, metabolism, and weight loss," all areas Oprah needed to learn about.

In the period before she took serious steps to lose and control weight, she was the butt of many a joke written not only in the lighter sections of newspapers—style sections, gossip columns, humorous essays—but also in business and financial news. From the moment she became known as a television host in Chicago, she became an easy target. From 1986 on, the language about size became less and less flattering as she gained more fans and was seen by competitors as a challenge; she was described as "hefty," or "heftier," "zaftig" (frequently), "Fat City," and a type of brash character who'd help herself to all the fattening snacks in a neighbor's refrigerator. In one of his columns, the humorist Art Buchwald describes family discussions, phone calls, and news bulletins that circulated about Oprah's weight gains or losses. In the business news, a well-known woman of the financial world had her weight compared to Oprah's. Even Internet humor found Oprah a good subject, calling her a virus that could shrink or expand a hard drive.

Oprah's weight, having become her greatest source of unhappiness, led her from one so-called cure to another. On numerous occasions, she went to spas when she wanted to lose weight in a controlled environment. In such a place, she met and hired Bob Greene. He and Oprah became acquainted in the summer of 1992, when he was a fitness director for a spa in Telluride, Colorado. Greene had heard of Oprah, but he'd never even seen her show. When he ran a health and fitness program at a hospital in South Florida, he suddenly began to get a large number of calls about the weight loss classes he conducted. People who had watched an Oprah show about the liquid diet that resulted in a loss of 67 pounds were eager to join Greene's classes. Oprah's most dramatic television demonstration, pulling a cart of 67 pounds of fat across the stage, had a strong impact on the television audience; in spite of the fact that Oprah's show focused on the results of a liquid diet, one aftermath of that program was the many calls about fitness to Greene from Florida residents. Oprah was not among the callers; she still believed in the efficacy of the liquid diet and had not become committed to exercise.

Greene didn't believe in the lasting effect of a liquid diet, certain Oprah would not remain thin once she returned to normal eating. Within a year, he was proved right. She had regained the weight, plus more poundage. Because every event featuring Oprah seems to be of national interest, the story of her fall, the journey from sleek to fat, was broadcast everywhere. Among the results were more phone calls from prospective clients for Greene's health and fitness program in Florida and, predictably, many other exercise facilities.

Two years later Greene changed jobs, moving from Florida to Colorado, which he chose because he preferred the mountains of the West to the ocean and flat countryside of Florida. Shortly after beginning work at Telluride, a new spa and resort, he met Oprah. Even though her purpose in going to the spa was to become more fit and lose weight, their meeting was an unlikely scenario, inasmuch as she was once again self-conscious about her weight, and he, as someone who didn't even own a television set, had little interest in that media.

By then Oprah had given up the Optifast liquid diet and was attempting to control her weight by eating the meals prepared by Rosie. But diet alone was not doing what she wanted, nor needed. In the three weeks that she stayed at Telluride she lost 10–12 pounds and, on leaving, she told Greene she'd be back.

In 1995, the book *Make the Connection: Ten Steps to a Better Body—and a Better Life* was published. Because it was intended to be seen as a joint effort, even though it was not quite equal, the authors' names are listed as Bob Greene and Oprah Winfrey, and the picture on the book jacket is of both of them. Yet some writers refer to it as "Oprah's book." In fact, it is Greene's book, but no matter how wise and useful his training and philosophy are, Greene's fabulous successes would not have occurred without the association with Oprah.

The first part of the book, 32 pages, is called "Oprah's Story." That section, as well as Greene's introduction, describes their meeting, her struggles with weight, and what both of them learned while working together. Before the end of the three-week period when they first met, Greene tells the reader, he learned a number of things about Oprah. Much of this, however, is applicable to many people who have the same goals: Oprah has physical stamina, a necessity because of the amount of work that must be put into exercise, and she understands healthful eating, inasmuch as Rosie Daley had by then been her chef for several years. And he says that will power, a major part of Oprah's character, is essential to bring about change. Without that quality, the difficult task will fail. It is a central link to understanding the hold emotions have to weight.

The pain and disappointment associated with weight control became evident in the many photos of Oprah scattered throughout the book, demonstrating the old cliché that one picture is worth a thousand words: thin, thinner, fat, fatter; running and preparing for a major marathon, four and a half hours at that beginning time. Ultimately—success, shown through the last set of pictures of a smiling, beautiful Oprah with her boyfriend Stedman Graham.

Two problems plaguing Oprah are not uncommon. She, like many people, does not have a strong metabolism, and she has always used food as a compulsive reaction to pressures and unhappiness in life. Eating, Greene points out, frequently comes from stress rather than hunger. As he observed Oprah's lifestyle, he learned about the different ways she'd break the dieters' rules. Snacking, eating out often, and eating the "wrong" kinds of food, celebrating every possible occasion, and doing so with foods that put the weight on. Eating when things went well, and eating when things went badly. Eating with friends who saw no reason for her to follow diet rules, and lacking the ability to say "no" to friends who always wanted to go out for a meal or entertainment.

Although Greene's book focuses on Oprah, the facts he provides about the issues of weight seem applicable to anyone who had struggled with it for long periods of time. Generally, diet books and programs speak of the problems that connect to weight, and, paradoxically, when they speak of loss they also emphasize gain, the gain of controlling our lives, the gain of confidence that comes with self-respect and self-love. Greene personalizes these matters by referring to the problems Oprah had to face. Many of them are universal, though some are seemingly unrelated. Greene speaks frankly, as Oprah does, of the ways friends undermined Oprah's efforts to lose weight, but Oprah also shows concern about fans who had adverse reactions to her shedding pounds. This led her to do a show about those people who feel they've been left behind when she, or someone close to the viewer has been more successful in weight loss.

Greene doesn't deal with dissociated or subsidiary topics, even though the behavioral response may be similar. He is an exercise physiologist, not a psychologist. He doesn't discuss certain types of responses or reactions by one's friends, colleagues, partners, or companions to changes in someone else's weight loss. She tells readers that she learned through trial, error, and suffering that each of us must bring about the alterations we want and not, as she put it, "give over our power to others" to direct our lives either because we are weak or because we want to please them. A major part of change is self-acceptance; to achieve that, she emphasizes, we also must become aware of who and what we are. Nevertheless, differences can come about only if we are willing to work on them. She writes in Greene's book that there have been occasions when she was so exhausted by exercise she wanted to scream. Exercising, she complained, is a never-ending ordeal. Greene, however, didn't and doesn't accept that, insisting one has to think of exercise as renewal; to understand that exercise, as with other elements in life, provides good days and less good days. An important effect rarely mentioned is the inspiration of a success story on many other people, those who accept us as we accept ourselves.

With exercise, an individual must do enough to bring about change. Along the way and over the years, Oprah had become discouraged, believing exercise didn't work for her because she had reached a point where she couldn't lose any weight. However, when she met Greene in 1993 he quickly analyzed her problems, inasmuch as dietary restrictions and exercise weren't helping; he discovered that for her it is necessary to exercise not only daily but more intensely in order to be able to improve and control her metabolism. He advised her also to exercise in the morning hours before the working day begins.

As a result of Greene's requirements, Oprah had to find a new routine that would allow her to fit in exercise and all that follows before the taping of her shows. Her days are long and arduous, but exercise helps her, in spite of the fact that she sometimes feels pain. With the taping of two or three shows each day, she has to awaken at five, exercise, shower, have her hair washed and set, and be made up by the time of the early morning taping at nine. And, in addition to those activities, she runs her company, goes to endless meetings, and travels a great deal. Yet in spite of her glamorous appearance in public, her fabulous clothes, glowing makeup, and eye-catching hairdos, she has been described by interviewers as someone who is not driven by the vanity some stars possess, and has on occasion met with world-famous people in her studio in old clothing, unset hair, and no cosmetics.

When she first started with Bob Greene, she began walking at what some walkers might consider a slow pace, that is, 17 minutes a mile, but she was able to bring that number down to 13 minutes a mile, then 8 minutes a mile, and soon she graduated to jogging. She can maintain her weight in fast walking, but jogging is essential for her to lose pounds. Her need for daily intense exercise means walking, lifting weights, jogging, or working out on a treadmill. She now says that exercise is essential for her both physically and emotionally in spite of time pressure or pain. Therefore, she states in Greene's book and elsewhere, even on vacation, she keeps up the same routine, training on a treadmill, walking, or jogging.

Make the Connection develops through a series of steps that a dedicated exerciser must follow, and along with the list of those requirements are comments by Oprah, many of them personal and confessional responses to Greene's prescriptions. For example, when he stipulates in "Step Four" that the individual must follow a balanced and low-fat diet, Oprah again reminds the reader, as she did in Daley's book, that nobody in her family knew anything about low-fat foods when she was growing up. Nothing, including vegetables, was cooked without fat. Once weight became a burden in her life she had to learn about calories, amounts of food, and acceptable snacks; about the role of alcohol in diets—forgo it entirely or drink very, very little; to avoid even healthful snacks late in the evening; and to drink large amounts of water throughout the day. But water, she tells the reader, is a problem for her—she didn't and still doesn't like water in any form, not even when it is flavored. She needed to establish certain individual routines in following the rules involving water. Just as she won't snack or eat after a certain hour, she won't drink water after six in the evening if she wants to sleep through the night.

The matter of water typically lent itself to Oprah's quick humor. It appeared when she spoke of her adjustment to water drinking at the beginning of her exercise program with Greene. In Indiana, where she owns a country house, while running with her trainer, she had to stop several times, and with no rest rooms on a country road, she used the wayside bushes. But even then, conscious of the ever-present photographers who dog her every activity, she thought of the possible outcome of being photographed while in that informal pose. Anyone who snapped that kind of picture of her, she told us, could retire on the proceeds earned.

Oprah, always the assiduous journal writer, keeps a record of her progress and failures in most activities. As a result, she has detailed her acceptance and pursuit of many of Greene's philosophical concepts. He talks about the joy of living, much like Smith but through different means, and he challenged Oprah to find joy rather than constant stress in her daily activities. Up to then she says that she thought of her happiest and most fulfilling time as that when she was making the movie *The Color Purple*. However, Greene wanted her to set a goal that would renew her and allow her to find happiness in other ways. During the years they have worked together she has written that she has taken on parts of his philosophy, attempting to find joy by living in each moment. Thus began a program of physical training that led to her delight in physical achievement.

In 2002 Simon and Schuster published a follow-up book by Greene called *The Get with the Program Guide to Good Eating*, which became number 12 among the top 50 books on the best-seller list in the week of January 2003. In its brief description of the new how-to book, the newspaper *USA Today* noted that the work consists of a program for eating, providing recipes that are intended to increase energy. Unlike his earlier book, this one has neither photos of Oprah nor any references to her. However, Greene's connection to Oprah remains strong; he continues as her expert in health and fitness in many areas, a member of her "Lifestyle Makeover Team," as well as a writer for both O and Oprah's online program.

Once Greene's guidance became part of her life, it had the desired effect. When Oprah became fit enough to move on to jogging from walking, she began to accept the possibility of racing suggested by Greene. By necessity, that is, her own tight scheduling, she went from jogging to running to participating in a half-marathon. Finally, as a marker and goal for her fortieth birthday, she decided she would compete in the Marine Corps Marathon in Washington, D.C. In some running events, various world-class celebrity runners are paid to attend, but the Marine Corps Marathon, a different type of program, is known as "The People's Marathon," in which nobody receives remuneration. Before the big day she hiked on difficult trails, such as those in the Grand Canyon, and participated in various short races; she followed a regimen of water sports—

swimming, kayaking, jet-skiing; she even began to use Rollerblade skates; and she found both the courage and stamina to ride an elephant. The Marines at Quantico who prepare for the run as one of their special projects spend many months getting in shape. For Oprah, a middle-aged woman unaccustomed to strenuous exercise before she began her training with Greene, it took two years of preparation.

Oprah ran 25 miles in the 1995 marathon and reached the finishing line. Cheered on by many watchers and other runners, she was also encouraged by two reporters from the *National Enquirer*. Never before, she claims, had she engaged in conversation with similar journalists. But these two rooted for her, tallying the miles, and urged her on as she covered the distance. Tearful and joyous at the conclusion, she says that she found it one of the unforgettable moments of her life. Because of Bob Greene, who enabled her to participate in and complete the marathon, she had lost 85 pounds. After the famed marathon, Oprah participated in other runs where the purpose was to raise money for charity, to help in the struggle against cancer—breast and ovarian—and AIDS.

Over a period of time Oprah began to work with a group of people for a series of programs that were called "Get Moving with Oprah." The fundamentals were learning about becoming fit through exercise and healthful eating. Their country walks became a feature of the series.

To become fit Oprah had to "get real," an expression favored by Greene, and also by Phil McGraw, the psychologist maven who appeared regularly on Oprah's program for several years; he also writes a monthly column in her magazine. Greene appears only occasionally on Oprah's programs, but he is a popular guest who also writes pieces for her magazine as well as a weekly "Oprah Online" column. Greene's philosophy of "getting real" is a task encompassing both body and mind. The so-called correct way is to maintain the exercise program. Eating is synonymous with sensible eating and snacking—one should eat omelets made from egg whites, not yolks; soups that eschew cream; rice cakes or pretzels instead of cookies or pie; potatoes that are baked instead of fried; popcorn that is served absolutely plain—air popped without butter; and, of course, fruits and vegetables. Furthermore, Greene stresses, one must recognize that eating is not a spree but three daily meals equal in size. Although Oprah has not always been able to stick with the rules—she did, after all, confess to consuming large amounts of pie and gaining weight during her ordeal in the Texas beef case. However, Oprah says that she has learned, as an overall concept, that life often is a struggle, bringing with it a mixture of good and bad days. Keeping fit, she now recognizes, is giving yourself permission to accept self-love.

To emphasize her newfound wisdom about food, weight, and beauty, her magazine frequently focuses on health-related matters; for example, the theme of the August 2002 issue of O was "Learning to Love Your Body." With every issue of the magazine the final essay, written by Oprah, is always entitled "What I Know for Sure." In that August column, which was even more personal than usual, she began with a headline that urged everyone to follow her example by accepting "the body you've been given." and "love what you've got." That is the only advice given in the piece; the focus is on her own struggle to reach the nirvana of acceptance.

Oprah tells us that she reached the state of calm approval of her physical being after her confrontation with fears about her heart. With a new and honest assessment of her body came a vow to take care of her heart as well as a pledge to accept her entire self from head to toe: her face with its lines beneath her eyes, the broadness of her nose, and the fullness of her lips. She ends the essay and issue with the powerful declaration that her "struggle is over," and at last she has "made peace" with her body.

Tabloids continue to watch Oprah relentlessly. In addition to stories about her weight and health, one recent story told of planned surgical procedures to improve her appearance; others reported great unhappiness. A variety of reasons were given. The writer of one article claimed that there had been a drop in the numbers of fans for Oprah's television programs and asserted that the magazine O was in even worse shape. However, a glance at the number of ads in each issue of the magazine proves their popularity. In fact, the consumer appeal of O as well as several other popular magazines is shown by the large amount of additional advertising linked to those magazines in a supplement published by Lincoln cars.

Personal as well as professional problems are also attributed to Oprah's so-called unhappiness. A so-called friend ascribed it to the introduction of Dr. McGraw's new television show. Because Oprah was responsible for his great success on her programs, she was under stress to see him succeed on his own, stated this person, because Oprah, reputedly believed that it affected her own reputation. That type of backroom gossip seems a rather flimsy excuse for the supposed "depressed" state of mind attributed to her. After all, she has helped make many a career, and it is difficult to believe that the possibility of a failed show would have a significant effect on her. Few people have had the opportunity and exposure given Dr. Phil by Oprah, who made him into a nationally—perhaps internationally—recognized figure, and the possibility of failure seems extremely remote at the current time.

The real or fictional personal problems described generally involve her longtime relationship with Stedman Graham, their ups and downs, and the stories usually blame Oprah for putting her career and other people before him. Matters of weight are generally invoked as well. Inevitably in each article, a warning bell is sounded that she is on a road that can only lead to a suspiciously undefined doom. Yet all of these reports are alternated in issues with such headlined articles about the long-term plans of Stedman and Oprah.

However, Oprah herself writes about accepting her flaws, physical and emotional, and also about her desire to live life to its fullest.

Chapter 7

O, THE CHOICE OF
WOMEN EVERYWHERE

Three publications, called "vanity magazines" by *Washington Post* food writer Candy Saigon dominated the women's market for several years: those of Martha Stewart (*Martha Stewart Living*), Oprah Winfrey (*O, The Oprah Magazine*), and Rosie O'Donnell (*Rosie*). Although everyone eagerly awaited the first of these, Martha Stewart's *Living*, Oprah's magazine has been more successful from the very beginning. The three of them, but particularly Stewart and Winfrey, always demonstrated strong qualities in all their undertakings, so that the magazines were expected to do well. Yet other women celebrities who also launched magazines during the same period foundered in their attempts after a short period of time: Ivana Trump, whose magazine *Ivana* went under almost immediately, and Tina Brown, who left her much-praised and prominent editorship at the *New Yorker* to start *Talk* but had poor notices from the onset, in spite of an inordinate amount of puffery from the publishing company. The failure rate for start-ups in magazines is extremely high; even John F. Kennedy, Jr.'s *George* was on the ropes just before Kennedy's tragic death in a plane crash. The great interest and affection the public held for him since his infancy could not save his magazine.

Like Oprah, Rosie began as a television star. However, after six years, Rosie left the playing field of television in May 2002. That event was soon followed by her departure from magazine publishing, in September 2002. Rumors had been circulating from early on about problems between her and the publisher of her magazine. Her exit from the magazine world, though, was nothing like the earlier move from television. In fact they were polar extremes. In contrast to the fiasco that marked the end of

Rosie's involvement with the magazine, her talk show was so popular that she was known as "the Queen of Nice," although not everyone agreed with that description. When the early announcement had been made of Rosie's joining the ranks of magazine chiefs, *Forbes*, after calling attention to the hierarchy with the line "First Martha, then Oprah, now Rosie," called her "opinionated," whereas Oprah's "touch" was dubbed "inspirational" by *Time* when her magazine first came out. Only a month after Rosie's retirement from the show, she proved herself to be not only opinionated but also determined to wipe the slate clean—or break it—as she scorned both the title and image that she'd previously enjoyed. Claiming "the bitch ain't so nice anymore," she began to take on other roles, including that of stand-up comic, returning, in part, to the type of comedy work she had done at the beginning of her career, except that her early comedy routines were much more wholesome than the later ones. The debate seems to continue among insiders and outsiders, in the manner of one *People*'s headline next to Rosie's photo: "Naughty or Nice?" Her friend Merv Griffin, who knows her from her early stand-up comedy days, has claimed that he always knew Rosie would be a success. As a mentor of Rosie's, who is said to have given her advice on every move she's made in her career, he maintains that he is convinced she is still a player, and he appears to be right. Her career doesn't seem to be floundering, in spite of ongoing lawsuits. Immediately after the brouhaha, in December 2002, Rosie was master of ceremonies at a gala in Manhattan for New York Women in Film. Newspapers and magazines still regard her as a star, and she remains highly visible.

The magazine *Rosie*, inaugurated in April 2001, a year after the first appearance of *O*, was a replacement for the 125-year-old *McCall's*, which had been losing millions in recent times. Where the original nineteenth-century *McCall's* focused on selling dress patterns of James McCall, a tailor, it underwent multiple reincarnations over the years, and the last one bore no resemblance to any earlier issues. When the publishing company, Gruner and Jahr—a division of Bertlesmann, an enormous German multimedia group and their staff closed down the old publication, name and all, they searched for a viable new magazine to take its place. Obviously seeking to emulate the success of the other two publications, *O* and *Martha Stewart Living*, they focused on Rosie O'Donnell as someone who would be strong competition to both. After all she was famous, funny, and popular, and she showed some of the same personality traits of Martha and Oprah: strength, determination, and staying power with audiences. Gruner and Jahr believed, as Hearst did with Oprah, they would have a ready-made group of subscribers from the television audience.

For a short period of time the two stars, Rosie and Oprah, seemed to be almost in lockstep: with a presence in television, magazines, and even books. Oprah's book choices, however, were more far-ranging than Rosie's, who limited her picks to children's books. Even with her work on television and her magazine, Rosie always concentrated much effort on children. She has adopted children and at the age of 40, along with her partner of five years, Kelli Carpenter, 35, became the mother of a new baby, to whom Kelli gave birth as a result of artificial insemination. Rosie was in the delivery room on November 29, 2002, for the arrival of their daughter Vivi.

Although it was said when *McCall's* became available that O'Donnell herself was behind the resolution to take over the magazine, hawking the idea was actually the decision of Rosie's business manager/brother-in-law, Dan Crimmins, and her lawyer, Philip Howard. The two persuaded Dan Brewster, the CEO of Gruner and Jahr, that a Rosie magazine would be something of a gold mine in what now seems to be a popular classification, "celebrity-as-brand," a description that appeared to be original with Stedman Graham, whose book *Build Your Own Life Brand* focuses primarily on celebrities, the most important of whom is Oprah. One wonders whether a combination of his terminology, narrative, and examples influenced the Rosie group. Whatever the impetus, the outcome was seen by a journalism professor at the University of Mississippi as an almost predictable disaster. Professor Samir Husni, who annually publishes a *Guide to New Consumer Magazines*, describes the Gruner and Jahr group as selling "their soul" to the television star as they looked "for a quick fix" for their problem. On the other hand, Judith Newman of *Vanity Fair* magazine writes that Dan Brewster, unlike other "magazine barons," was enthralled by the proposal.

Both the publisher and O'Donnell had an equal stake in the undertaking, and each was motivated to succeed. At the beginning *Rosie* seemed to fulfill the publisher's hopes, with strong sales and increasingly lucrative numbers of ads. The magazine's format was mostly standard: crafts, health, and food. Causes were also discussed, an unusual addition to the typical women's magazine. Some controversial elements, both political and social, were included. One particular topic that Rosie and the magazine skirted was the matter of the gay life, a life that Rosie led quietly, although she didn't actually keep it secret. In fact, many people in the entertainment industry knew that Rosie was a lesbian, but the public had little knowledge, and most of her audience and readership apparently were unaware of it. After all, in the main, Rosie projected a traditional image of family life as the adoptive mother of several children. However, in spite of

hints and whispers, and after years of being circumspect about her private
affairs and sexual predilections, Rosie went public with her autobiography, *Find Me*.

Since then, Rosie has made no attempt to hide her sexual preference.
She is certainly not the first or only entertainer to make such an announcement, but it may have caused falling ratings for what was considered a "family show." Her tell-all book had preceded by a month her exit
from her television show. Soon after publication of her book, sales of the
magazine began to fall precipitously. Few critics specifically ascribe the
drop in newsstand purchases to Rosie's so-called outing but rather to her
social and political views. Yet, she has always held these views, and they
did not appear to offend the readership previously. Soon, stories of wars
between Rosie and her staff were being told, and then information about
the hostile relationships of Rosie and the publishers surfaced.

In the midst of the battles between them, the star wrote an inflamma-
tory column for the magazine. Though never printed because of preven-
tive actions taken by the publisher, it was leaked to the press. In an article
that was variously described by journalists as rambling, incoherent, and
accusatory, Rosie wrote about the interference of the publishers in her
management of staff. Yet, with the unraveling of the publication, staffers
have told stories of Rosie's unavailability, of sending in as a substitute for
her presence at the office a relative of her live-in partner to interpret her
"vision," and such viciousness in her behavior that at least one staffer said
she feared for her own safety.

Part of Rosie's unprinted statement declared that she had wanted to be
a cooperative member of the group; but she said that had not worked, and
although she did not want to be a "control-[expletive]...like Oprah and
Martha," she would become one. She would be as uncompromising as
they are, she avowed. But control belonged to the publishers, and Rosie
resigned after firing off salvos against their actions. The publishers then
retaliated publicly in stronger language, blaming her for destroying the
magazine and violating her contract. When the partnership of Gruner
and Jahr filed a $100 million lawsuit for breach of contract, Rosie submit-
ted a countersuit. The December 2002 issue of *Rosie* was its last. Described
by *Washington Post* writer Peter Carlson as an "awful" magazine, it is
clearly finished, having lost millions of dollars, and whether something
else will take its place seems unlikely. Neither side was awarded any dam-
ages and the case was dismissed.

Rosie's volatility should have been recognized by the publishers. After
all, she has always been outspoken. Further, she has not always recognized

contradictions in her stated views. As a television host she shared the spotlight with one celebrity after another, and, according to a *Newsweek* reporter, Rosie wept on some occasions, gushed at other times, hugged Madonna, whom she proclaimed her dearest friend, yet announced that she wanted her magazine to be about "real women," not celebrities. Perhaps it was all about personality, as stated in a magazine advertisement to attract subscribers, "*Rosie* is the magazine with personality." The magazine certainly could lay claim to personality when it featured pictures of Rosie sick with a staph infection. That July 2001 issue made a large impression, albeit a critical one. Her story and photos followed Rosie's dictum about showing "real" people, but they upset her publishers and caused a humorous stir in the press.

Like Oprah, Rosie has said that she was enthralled by the television shows she saw as a youngster. Rosie, however, had much more freedom and opportunity to view them than Oprah did. In that and other ways, their early years had no resemblance to one another. Where Oprah's childhood in Mississippi consisted of years of loneliness and deprivation, Rosie grew up in a large Irish Catholic home and New York neighborhood with a mother who was beautiful, funny, and involved with her church, her children, and all of their activities. Rosie spent her after-school hours with her mother watching variety shows as well as sitcoms. Some of their childhood experiences, however, were similar, in that both as young children had a wall of protection, Oprah by her grandmother, and Rosie by her mother.

Rosie's sense of security changed when her mother died, and the household of five children was left without an anchor. Her father could not and did not cope, was usually unavailable, and became an alcoholic. Oprah went to live elsewhere with a mother she hardly knew. In comparison to Oprah's childhood years spent in Milwaukee from 6 to 14, in a dysfunctional family with an unmarried mother who did not protect her from predators and sexual abuse, Rosie's life seems relatively easy. Nevertheless, at a time of adolescence, when Oprah at last had a take-charge father to guide her life, Rosie's father proved inadequate, so that she was very much on her own. Oprah went on to college, whereas Rosie dropped out after trying the academic world briefly, with a year at Dickinson and six months at Boston College. Oprah was "discovered" by Nashville radio and television and then Baltimore television, but Rosie, with almost no support or encouragement at home or among friends or others in show business, had to find her way over a period of several years through the comedy circuit.

In 1986, when Oprah was just becoming a household name, and Rosie was performing at a Los Angeles club, Rosie's comments about and impersonation of Oprah became a favorite with audiences. Everyone and everything were fair game in that period. Rosie's comedy skit about Oprah's white/black persona, while questionable in several ways, nevertheless is not very different from anti-Oprah statements made over the years by members of the black community. In those years few could imagine that there would come a period when the two women would be at the top of the media world, each with a television show and magazine bearing her own name, names so famous they're known around the world.

In time, Rosie became a television star, first in a short running sitcom, then in a television movie, and finally as a television host of a daytime talk show. Ironically, her studio was one previously used by Phil Donahue, the talk show host Oprah put out of business. Not as successful as Oprah, Rosie's show was not actually a rival to Oprah's—the shows had different time slots and were shown on different channels—nor was her decision to retire from the show the result of competition; neither was her resignation from the magazine bearing her name. Yet columnists constantly suggested that they were competitors.

One element common to the early backgrounds of O'Donnell, Stewart, and Winfrey, their need and desire to succeed—to become rich and famous—seems to have driven the three of them to legendary heights in the business world and on television. Unlike Rosie and Oprah, however, Stewart came from a two-parent family who lived to see her phenomenal success. Yet, with an angry, thwarted, cold, and uncommunicative father, Martha always had an overwhelming need to prove to him she could achieve wealth, recognition, and fame.

Martha Stewart's fall from grace came in 2002 with the allegation that she had violated the rules of insider stock trading. The stock in question was that of major pharmaceutical company ImClone, which was developing a new cancer drug. However, early reports about the drug turned out to be unfavorable, leading those with inside information to unload the stock. Martha Stewart allegedly heard about the upcoming announcement of the Food and Drug Administration (FDA) from her broker, and Stewart had him sell the stock, reputedly for $200,000. Some financial writers have pointed out that Stewart was a very small player in all of this, and some have protested her so-called trial in the media. Her defense was that she'd instructed her broker to sell the stock at any time it fell below a certain price, and the sale had nothing to do with inside information. Stewart's situation, however, has been murkier.

Numerous speculative stories about Stewart were printed because television commentators and comedians seemed to find her situation too interesting to ignore. From the outset, Stewart, who had been a stockbroker in her early years, maintained her innocence in all the dealings. Nevertheless, the fact that she'd been a broker is seen as something of an Achilles' heel by various critics, who claim with such a background she had to be aware of an illegality. Before all this happened, Stewart headed a huge company built on revenues from a television show, magazines, and her own line of products sold at K-mart stores. The estimated worth of her organization, Martha Stewart Living Omnimedia, was $800 million, in addition to her own personal fortune. In fact the considerable amount of her wealth led her defenders to point to the comparatively insignificant sum of money involved in the stock sale. On the other hand, those antipathetic to Stewart claimed that she was simply greedy.

In early June 2003, a federal grand jury indicted Stewart, charging she'd lied and misled investigators about her role in the stock sale, which had taken place 18 months earlier. Although federal prosecutors and the Manhattan U.S. attorney disagreed about the actions to be taken, the Securities Exchange Commission (SEC) brought a five-part civil complaint against her for insider trading, which was not a criminal charge. Many lawyers disagreed about the charges and ramifications, as did other experts, journalists, and members of the public. In a June 8, 2003, poll taken by CNN, 68 percent of the viewers' responses were pro-Stewart.

Not a few commentators have pointed to the fact that nobody was hurt by Stewart's stock sale, and they have compared it to the recent criminal activities of huge companies that destroyed lives, jobs, savings, and pensions of thousands of people. A number of journalists made light of her actions as minor offenses. One writer, Libby Copeland, in something of a tongue-in-cheek article, says Stewart has a "fatal flaw": she was sloppy about the details of her relationship with her viewers—and that hypocrisy soils her image. Further, some Stewart champions, mostly women, believe the attacks on her have a distinctly antifemale tinge, a hostility directed against a strong, aggressive, and successful woman; the accusations, her supporters say, would never be leveled against a male in the same situation.

When the indictment was announced, Stewart stepped down as chairman and CEO of her company and at the same time published in the *New York Times* a full-page advertisement defending her position. She also went on the Internet to do the same. Since the beginning of 2001 her picture has not been on the cover of *Martha Stewart Living* nor was her name used in Omnimedia's food magazine, *Everyday Living*, even though food writers reproducing recipes from the magazine or praising it always mention Stewart's name. Even though Stewart denied all the allegations of insider trading, her company's stock fell abruptly, to a small percentage of its value. The popularity of her earlier magazine also went into a spin. For the first time since its inception, the media and retailing company showed a quarterly loss at the end of 2002. Where, in the previous year, the company had earned more than $5.7 million in profits, revenues for the last quarter of 2002 were down by $2 million. An even greater drop was anticipated, with a possible 25 percent fall in advertising revenue. The first quarter's report for 2003 showed a loss of 15 percent in revenue and the projection for the second quarter in Martha Stewart Living Omnimedia was not promising. What the future of Stewart's empire will be, including the fate of her magazine, remains to be seen. A jury found her guilty in January 2004. Plea bargaining might keep Stewart out of prison, but many expect her to pay a significant fine, and business pundits speculate about her future.

Yet her products are still being marketed, particularly in K-mart where, it is claimed, the sales of her products are still up, and she is shown frequently in television ads touting them. As a gesture of support for Martha—and hope that the sales of her merchandise will help them—K-mart would not allow the sale of the tabloid *Globe*, which featured a story based on an unfriendly book about her. The front-page headline of the paper stated "Mean Martha Exposed." Stewart remains a big ticket news item, as if commentators can't get enough of the story. One instance is seen in fashion columnist Robin Givhan's very lengthy article about Stewart's style of dress, calling it dowdy and dull. The reporter's criticism of Stewart's clothing elicited protests from readers of the *Washington Post* a few days later. All of them question Givhan's high-fashion values for Stewart, a middle-aged woman in years and build, one who makes products for the lower end of the market, K-mart, although for that company her goods are at the top of their line. One letter writer expressed trust that she'd never be caught committing a "high-profile crime," but if she should and then be found out, she hoped that Givhan wouldn't be the person writing about her "go-to-jail ensemble."

In the effort to stem losses, the assertion that advertising has increased in Martha's magazine is made periodically by the company, in contradiction to their acknowledgment of a 20-percent drop in sales at newsstands and the same percentage fall in revenue coming in to the publishing division.

Famous stars are known for their ability to sell products and magazines. Apparently, most buyers are able to separate products and magazines from the blemished names and personal life of many well-known entrepreneurs. Surely that's been the case with entertainers in various fields. Perhaps, though, it is the very taint of scandal that catches the public and the shoppers' eye. Business assessors opine that media chiefs will continue to search for more stars who will attract purchasers, and celebrity names are floated periodically in the news.

A cold-blooded movie presentation on television of Stewart's life story may well add fodder to her already damaged reputation. Not everyone, however, including the starring actress and various journalists, agree about the biases of the television story. Writing in his *Washington Post* column "Washington Investing," Jerry Knight labeled the film "a surreal soap opera." Mockingly describing the stereotypical characterizations, he compared the television movie to two very popular series of yesteryear: *Dynasty* and *Dallas*, and found similarities to *Cinderella* and *Alice in Wonderland*.

Knight blamed the ever-expanding clamor on Stewart's arrogance and failure to pay attention to details—a shocking failure, given her reputation for being obsessive about details. Suggesting a surprising naiveté in Stewart, Knight speculated that she didn't realize that the government, that is, the SEC, was "playing hardball with [her] because she's a celebrity." If that was so, there was a certain blindness in Stewart's failure to understand the pitfalls of the renown she has sought all her life.

Although circulation has fallen for Stewart's magazine, it may or may not be attributable to the publicity about her stock trading. Significantly, in spite of the fact that advertising is up, news reports in late 2002 also point to somewhat poorer circulation for Oprah's magazine, which has never been touched by scandals of any sort. Neither Stewart's or O'Donnell's magazines, however, seem to have offered much of a challenge to Oprah's, even though all three were found on the same magazine racks in stores. Some of the largest grocery chains stocked both Stewart's and O'Donnell's magazines, sometimes one or the other, but inexplicably not Oprah's.

Comparisons and evaluations within the category are inevitable each time a new woman's magazine appears. Because one of the most popular drawing cards for women's magazines has always been the segment on food, it was inevitable that food editors such as Candy Saigon of the *Washington Post* would compare the food offerings of O, *Martha Stewart Living*, and *Rosie*. Saigon claimed that the magazines had different food personalities, listing the kind of food she'd choose to describe each. Thus, she said she thinks of a chili dog as representing *Rosie*; garlic mashed potatoes—an Oprah favorite—were also the food Saigon thought of as representative of the magazine *O*; and her choice for Stewart's magazine was a lemon verbena torte so elaborate that several lines of newsprint were needed to describe it.

Of the three choices, Saigon was somewhat dismissive of Rosie's type of so-called comfort food, but said that she preferred the recipes in Oprah's magazine to those of Martha, because they took less time to prepare, were more dependable, and were not as "labor-intensive." Because the style director of *O* develops her concept with the aid of nonstaff recipe originators and writers of cookbooks, the magazine has no food editors of its own, no test kitchen, and only a small food staff.

One of the most prominent bookseller chains in the country, Borders, features *O* so prominently it would be difficult to get through the purchasing line without seeing the magazine as a special display. Oprah has been a huge factor in the sale of books, a boon to writers, publishers, and bookstores, and even to discount and department stores such as Costco, Sam's Club, and Target, all better known for food items and other merchandise. A large number of bookstores carry her magazine, but many discount stores do not. Although such stores did not publicize Oprah's choices by dividing them from other books, most regular bookstores contained separate racks of Oprah's book selections. Her logo on books increased sales "tenfold," according to a report by Time Warner. The early books are no longer featured, but those that remain in print still carry the sticker announcing them as an Oprah choice, and now that Oprah is back in the business of touting books, albeit classics, logos are being affixed and sales are up once again. In fact her first choice of summer 2003, John Steinbeck's *East of Eden* quickly rose to the top of the paperback best-seller list.

Oprah's magazine was described by writer Patricia Sellers of *Fortune* as "the most successful magazine launch ever." Although it first appeared on U.S. newsstands in July 2000, it was expanded within the year to an international edition in June 2000. That edition is as glossy as the U.S. one and almost as huge. However, the subject matter is not entirely the same. A significant percentage is devoted to South African matters and people, with both black and white women as the readership. *O* is published jointly by the Hearst Corporation and Winfrey's Harpo Entertainment Group. Following its American inaugural issue of 322 pages of extremely large print with a run of 1.6 million copies, the magazine grew to a readership of two and a half million within a short period of time. With annual revenues topping $140 million, it is a considerable part of the Harpo empire, surprisingly profitable in an industry in which the majority of magazines rarely make a profit in the first years after their establishment. At a time when other longtime women's magazines have failed, O still continues to attract a significantly large number of new readers. The current paid circulation figure outperforms even such longtime female favorites as *Vogue*, although some of the designer brands and high-end automobiles advertised are the same. The items advertised, photographed, and recommended to readers are geared toward the purchaser at the upper-middle-income level: Tommy Hilfiger clothing for children; Calvin Klein and Estee Lauder perfumes. The majority of items for the home, crystal and elegant table settings, would not be found in low-end or discount shops.

Success of a high-powered publication does not come without dedication and tussles. Where, according to Gayle King, editor at large of the magazine, Oprah is obsessive about O, overseeing everything, even commas and exclamation points, numerous people have told of the amount of time she puts into work on it. But there also have been reports, though carefully squelched, of tension and problems in the staff. Shortly after the public introduction of the magazine, the newly appointed editor in chief, Ellen Kunes, resigned. Although Kunes stated she was resigning for "personal reasons," some Oprah watchers questioned that. Kunes was replaced very quickly by former chief editor of *Mirabella*, Amy Gross, who continues to hold that position.

From its inception, like many other magazines directed toward a female audience, O has followed a pattern of topics known to appeal to a specific group of women, those said to be more financially upscale than Oprah's daily television watchers. O also includes some regular features all its own, covering topics from cosmetics to books. Clearly, it is Oprah's magazine and at times she seems ubiquitous. Following her opening essay, "Here We Go," is an attractive calendar for the entire month, with photographs appropriate to the season. Thus, one year the offerings for the month of November featured knitting yarns in richly colored yarns of red and burnt orange, a teakettle and cups of hot tea, and an autumnal sunset scene; an August calendar pictured a mother and her two children bathing in the ocean. A featured statement by a recognizably famous person—such as Gandhi or James Baldwin—heads up the calendar, with aphorisms for most of the days. Every issue of the magazine has a different subject announced on the cover. Some that have appeared over a two-year period are: Friendship; Success; Creativity; Family; Intimacy; Fun; Confession; Adventure; Love Your Body; Stress Relief; You're Invited; Home; To Your Health; Love, Sex, and Dating; Communicate; Balance; Energy, Truth; Freedom; Couples; Strength, and Weight. Many seem to relate to topics that are dealt with on the television show. One story in the magazine, about the Andrea Yates tragedy, was also dealt with at length on television.

Both told of a mother who had murdered her children. The print focus was on the life and background of the young mother, who came from a family that suffered from numerous mental illnesses—bipolar disorder, depression, alcoholism. Yates attempted suicide twice, was hospitalized numerous times, suffered from hallucinations, was given antipsychotic medications that she discontinued, refused to practice birth control in spite of warnings from her physicians—and had more children. Her diagnosis of postpartum psychosis, not the temporary condition of postpartum depression, should have been a red flag to everyone concerned, but it was ignored or overlooked and calamity followed. The television program went into more detail with information provided by experts.

Each issue of the magazine brings advice of many kinds, much of it in Oprah's pieces, as well as in the regular monthly columns, and in articles by specialists on a particular subject. Oprah has been described as the national therapist, and the magazine seems to fulfill the same role. The style of O is personal, often confessional. Most of the problems of life find their way eventually onto the beautiful glossy spread, which features a photo of Oprah on the cover as well as many other photos of her inside. Sometimes the cover photo is duplicated in greater detail within the magazine. And, when a particularly beautiful picture of Oprah appears in newspapers and other magazines, it also is printed in O. On the night she accepted the Bob Hope Humanitarian Award, Oprah wore a stunning white silk gown that was photographed and talked about in a number of magazines, including her own. Over a period of several years, through photos alone, a reader may gain insight about the star's preferences in clothing, from casual shirts and pants to elegant hostess apparel. The same may be said about her hairdos: long, short, curly, straight, flipped, upturned.

When on occasion Oprah has been asked why only her picture is used on every cover, her answer has been somewhat ingenuous; it is to avoid the necessity of making choices of other people every month. Inside, however, in addition to the many pictures of Oprah, the photos are generally of celebrities—perhaps alongside a brief article by or about them. Background scenes of flowers, green fields, and blue water abound. Although a great many of the articles are about serious matters, others are about leisure activities, such as descriptions and photos of parties Oprah has given. One such happening was a garden party, labeled a "hat party" by Oprah. Close friends, plus people she works with were the invited guests pictured in their exquisite hats: Gayle King, Maria Shriver, Kate Forte (president of Harpo Films), Dianne Atkinson Hudson (executive producer of the *Oprah Winfrey Show*), and three other supervising senior producers. Held at the home of a friend in Montecito, California, the party is a tribute to the elegant life of the rich and famous. Against a backdrop of colors, flowers, and greenery are gorgeous shots of food—hors d'oeuvres, salad, a chicken main dish, drinks, and desserts. The table settings and linens are like the products that the star recommends in every issue, as well as on television. All of those are big business.

Among the invariable monthly articles, Oprah's "Here We Go," serves to introduce the theme treated in the majority of articles, most written by women. The advertisements and articles reinforce the view held by readers of Oprah herself as a woman not only of wisdom but also tenderheartedness, as, for example, a full-page picture in which she is shown hugging a woman; underneath it are two lines; the first reads, "Exercise your heart everyday," and beneath that are the words, "Watch the *Oprah Winfrey Show*." There is much so-called heart exercise in the magazine.

Every issue also features an interview in which Oprah talks to someone famous or important to her, people she knows well or only through reputation, but always those she admires. On occasion the interviews provide insight into Oprah herself, as they have in the discussions with two people for whom she has expressed her unconditional love: her closest friend of more than a quarter of a century, Gayle King, and Quincy Jones, a dear mentor. Oprah always credits her friends for the help they have given her in good times and bad. Although volumes have been written about the value of friendship, in the matter of friendship, Oprah adds her own take by quoting a favorite line from a favorite book, *Beloved*: the friend that matters is the "friend of the mind." In spite of her often-stated belief in self-reliance, she declares that "nobody can make it alone." She says that she can rely on her friends for honesty and grounding.

In the constant effort to provide multiple points of view—not only happy, positive ones—varied positions are shown in the articles printed in the magazine whenever possible. Thus, in an issue filled with testimonies to the value and importance of friendship, there is also a thoughtful piece on ending friendship: why, how and when it should happen. Not all friendships are forever, and one must face such realities honestly.

The magazine has included interviews with many different people since it was first published and not all of them are personal friends of Oprah—some others are famous figures, such as Condoleezza Rice. Like most of the people Oprah interviews, Rice spoke openly about her background and experiences. Rice, a contemporary of Oprah's, has had a very different kind of life. Yet there are some similarities. Both were born in the segregated South, Rice in Alabama, where she attended segregated schools until she reached the tenth grade and her family moved to Denver. Rice, the cherished daughter of a loving family, studied piano, expecting to become a concert pianist. Like Oprah, Rice has accomplished many firsts. She eventually became the first nonwhite provost at Stanford University and later security advisor to a president. The two women are similar not only in the fact of their remarkable accomplishments but also in their sense of self and confidence, in their ability to do what they set their minds on, and their strengths under pressure. Each is known throughout the world as making a mark on history.

Strength, but also his lack of fear of loss and death are qualities that Oprah talked about with former Mayor Rudy Giuliani when she interviewed him in January 2002. Giuliani was the subject of many news reports and interviews by an admiring, even worshipful public all during the fall of 2001. Having first met him at a memorial service at Yankee Stadium shortly after the September 11 attacks on New York, Oprah questioned him about his reactions, bravery, and leadership in the crisis and period following it. Unlike some of her other interviews, only briefly did this one deal with personal matters, and it was Giuliani who introduced the matter of his love affair with Judith Nathan, speaking of her as the woman who saw him through the most difficult period of his life. Oprah delicately skirted the matter of his very public romance while married to someone else and the publicity given to it for a long period of time by newspapers and magazines.

Unusual, even terrible, events propel people such as the mayor from their local setting into the national consciousness. With entertainers, who are frequent subjects for the media, it generally takes something out of the ordinary to bring about an Oprah interview, as it did in the case of Michael J. Fox, who became ill at the height of his career. When the actor left his very successful television show, he informed an affectionate and admiring public about his struggle with Parkinson's disease. The popular and successful young movie and television star, with a loving wife and family, had to change his direction in life. From that point on he established a research foundation, became a frequent speaker about the disease, and devoted himself completely to the national effort of combating the devastating illness. Giving an interview to Oprah in March 2002 became part of that effort, allowing Fox to share information about Parkinson's.

Illness and health are frequent subjects in O, so that when some particular spark catches the attention of the public, Oprah chooses to interview unusual people like Fox, whose strength and willpower in the face of a ravaging disease inspires others. At another time, in November 2002, seven months after the Fox interview, she talked with a childhood victim of muscular dystrophy, 12-year-old Mattie Stepanek. Mattie, whom Oprah has called her friend, was the only one of four children in his family to survive. After his four-year-old brother's death, Mattie began to write poetry at the age of three by dictating to his mother. As he grew older he called his poems "Heartsongs," considering them to be songs of hope. Although he was confined to a wheelchair and was unable to lead a normal childhood, he appeared very philosophic as he discussed death and heaven with Oprah. In surprisingly adult and sophisticated language, he spoke to Oprah of purpose and usefulness, attitudes that mirror her own. She responded by saying affectionately, "You're my guy." Oprah attended Mattie's funeral when he died in July 2004.

The subject of health is given much consideration in the magazine, not only as the theme of an issue. Every month the issue includes at least one article about health, and sometimes as many as four. The matter of weight, particularly, always a staple of women's magazines, gets much attention. Inasmuch as it seems the entire world watches Oprah's weight, O provides a forum to reveal her successes and failures, just as she has on her shows for years. In one issue she listed the many different diets she tried, and she spoke of the necessity of taking care of her body. At the same time, she became determined to accept what she had been given—her nose, her curves, and her lips. Since the time Bob Greene became her trainer, exercise has been a daily part of her life. Oprah encourages her readers and television viewers to emulate her healthy activities: to eat right and exercise, exercise, exercise. Even though she's always had remarkable vitality, exercise keeps her exceptionally fit. She includes photos of herself in her magazine as support for her articles and her urgings.

Some of the information provided in the health articles, though available in other written or televised form, by physicians, or on the Internet, often comes as news to readers. A piece on osteoporosis, an illness common to many women, pointed out that men, too, may unknowingly have the disease. Because large numbers of readers are concerned about the possibility of developing Alzheimer's, Oprah featured an article about it. Andrew Solomon's discussion, in "I Remember It, um, Well," told of memory loss and ways to prevent much of it—though noting that it's not possible to arrest it entirely. Current statistics reveal that the more education people have, the less apt they are to succumb to Alzheimer's disease. According to the magazine article, it is possible to do things to improve brain power. Scientists now believe the brain can grow new cells through use: reading, word games, training of the memory, and certain physical activities. Solomon passed on some further advice: get sufficient sleep, and avoid stress, alcohol, and smoking.

Each month, in addition to health matters, the magazine includes advice of all kinds. One example is the column of Suze Orman called "Financial Freedom," which provides a practical guide to the management of money. Orman, like several other contributors, answers questions of all kinds, primarily about money and investments. She occasionally moves into other areas, such as providing an executor's checklist for handling a will. Unhesitatingly, she tackles problems of modern American culture and mores in discussing important and sensitive issues. A central one is the way women control their own income. Traditionally, even when both partners in a marriage worked, they pooled their salaries. However, as the ratio of working women increased and people began to marry later, women became more independent and accustomed to handling their own finances. Orman looks at the situation from many perspectives, and advises women that they do not need permission to control the money they earn. She says that power shouldn't be apportioned according to the size of a paycheck, using another of Oprah's famous entreaties to women readers not to "give over [their] power."

Beauty, health, and style articles appear in every issue, as well as a self-help piece by Oprah called "Something to Think About." This column is a written exercise that lists numerous questions to be answered by the reader in the spaces provided. The self-help segment becomes a form of self-therapy as the reader follows the technique occasionally used by therapists, including Dr. McGraw in his monthly "Tell It Like It Is" column. He answers questions asked by individual readers, but his recommendations may be applied to a much wider audience. McGraw, who became a television star and author as a result of his exposure on the *Oprah Winfrey Show*, sometimes offers the same information in the magazine that appears in his book. In one column, "The Crossroads of You," for example, he covered a wide expanse of human needs in his list of seven critical choices most people make; briefly he discusses types of fulfillment, survival and security, love, self-esteem and expression.

Critics have faulted McGraw for what they have labeled "five-minute therapy," a charge he has said is unfair and incorrect. Much that he writes for the magazine is "getting real" about problems that may have touched many generations but also some that have come with modern living. One significant example is that of teenage sex. When O published an article about "Girls and Sex," McGraw expanded the discussion with a piece about boys and sex, adding valuable insights and information for parents and children alike. Perhaps it is his visibility that has evoked so much comment, but unlike his more audacious daily television show, his articles also fit into a long-established pattern of most women's magazines, and, in contrast to the critics, women readers—as well as his television viewers—are effusive in their praise of his work. It almost goes without saying that Oprah has been and continues to be one of those supporters.

Oprah also took up the matter of girls and sex, as she has before, particularly in speaking of her own traumatic introduction to sex. Although her story of those events is no longer news, she continues to identify with the troubling problems underlying teenage sex, believing the root causes are the same: the failure of parents to communicate, the fear of young people to reveal intimate occurrences, the distance between parents and children. Pervasive unhappiness and self-blame resulting from sexual activities become a pattern that is difficult to break.

In telling the world about herself, Oprah applies her own brand of therapy. More and more often, in recent years she has returned to memories of her own childhood, recalling her grandmother, who, in spite of her severity and rigidity, communicated unspoken affection to the little girl. Even though she was unaware then of her grandmother's love, the events of those early days have come back to her over time. Calling these realizations "Aha" moments, Oprah features others' descriptions of personal "Aha" moments in the magazine, as well. After years of trauma in various relationships, she began to recognize the gifts her grandmother gave her. Perhaps remembrance of things past—what one poet called "the eternal landscape"—serves her like the "grateful journal" she has advised young women to keep. Her own "Aha" moments and those of others take on the quality of epiphanies, the light of recognition.

Oprah has said that she believes in sharing, which is different from giving away control to anyone. Sharing helps others as well as ourselves. Sharing takes many forms, including talk, which is both sharing and healing, not whining or being humbled or defeated. Furthermore, taking responsibility is like a building block of character. Those who refuse to bow to silence and isolation elicit her admiration. Even when she tells of her heartbreaking youth she does it without self-pity because she has learned that all of us must be in charge of our own lives and find our own happiness. Everyone—she tells her readers—children and adults yearn for family and affection; children, particularly, deserve love and approval, but such longings are not always fulfilled. One must not grieve for what is not given but find another path. Whatever our achievement, success in life comes from learning to love and accept ourselves. Without that we are unable to love others.

Central messages such as these account for the affection and trust of women worldwide, and will continue to be the strengths of both the *Oprah Winfrey Show* and *O* magazine.

Chapter 8

INTO THE FUTURE

At the end of filming *The Color Purple*, Quincy Jones told Oprah, "Your future is so bright that it's going to burn your eyes." Oprah has repeated the statement at various times because it is clearly one she believes. She and other successful women that she has interviewed agree that this is a fortunate time in which to be living. Yet, it seems apparent that Oprah's temperament and will would have made her a leader even in earlier days because, as she says again and again, she believes in taking charge of self, of being responsible for our own lives. Although she isn't blinded to the reality of problems that often appear insurmountable, she tells readers and audiences of her attempts to find ways to deal with difficulties. One such approach is in listening to a favorite gospel song called "Stand," which responds its own question "What do you give when you've given your all, and it seems you can't make it through?" with its refrain, "You just stand."

With the song serving metaphorically for the determination needed to overcome all adversity, like the Ancient Mariner of Coleridge's poem, she repeats her message whenever the occasion calls for it. Throughout her life she has found the strength to overcome hurdles, exhorting everyone to do the same. And even though she says that she didn't "set out to create" what she labels "this big life," she intends to meet all its challenges. In one forum or another, in speeches, writings, and programs, Oprah expresses her conviction that it is the journey that matters. In spite of the fact that her so-called big life provided almost everything, her optimism suggests "the best is yet to come." The spiritual side of her nature informs her of a mission, a responsibility to the world, and even the planet, to use her life to do good. It is little wonder that a journalist was led to write, "In America, there is **Oprah,** and then there's everyone else."

At Christmas in 2002, Oprah went to South Africa, a country she'd visited numerous times before. On that recent trip she provided gifts to 50,000 boys and girls from different provinces. Although the children were given jeans, T-shirts, balls, radios, and black dolls, something they'd never seen, what most of them cherished were sneakers that fit them for the first time in their lives, a revelation that touched Oprah as well as the team that distributed the items. The group consisted of people from the Oprah Winfrey Foundation, staff members, and friends, including boyfriend Stedman Graham. The Christmas show in 2003, broadcast from South Africa, had AIDS as its focus, the disease that has devastated and continues to devastate the African population.

Oprah had given money to girls' schools previously, and during the three weeks she spent in South Africa, ground was broken for a school that she financed, "The Oprah Winfrey Leadership Academy for Girls [in] South Africa." That school, scheduled to open in 2005, was to be the first of many, serving as a model for the others. Oprah talked of opening 12 schools for girls in Africa, as well as two in Afghanistan, and one in Mississippi. Oprah said that she intended to teach classes to the children via satellite from Chicago.

While in South Africa, Oprah and Stedman stayed at the home of Nelson Mandela, and she noted in her magazine that they had 29 meals with him. In July of 2003 she returned with a number of world-famous people, including former President Bill Clinton, Hillary Rodham Clinton, and their daughter Chelsea, to celebrate Mandela's eighty-fifth birthday. In describing the visit, Oprah proclaimed her thanks to God for what she "was born to see...to touch, hear, and feel that kind of happiness."

The question frequently asked is whether Oprah will continue with her daily television programs? Making movies? Acting? Directing? Producing? At the moment she has ruled out acting, but Oprah has been known to change her mind about career moves. Every time there are rumors about her retiring from her show in a certain year or at a certain age, she blithely moves on as if there has never been any doubt about her direction. Characteristically, Oprah, who loves poetry, quotes lines if they seem applicable to what she is saying; she does that when considering her own life and writing about the good luck of women born in America. Stressing their right to follow the path of choice, she admonishes them to "Use it," and adds a quotation from a favorite poet, Emily Dickinson: "Dwell in possibility." Her own way, now and in the future, seems to be just that.

As she told host Larry King, she continues to think of herself as "a woman in process." Her inclination hasn't changed from the lines of her theme song: "I believe I'll run on and see what the end will be."

At the conclusion of one of her personal "What I Know for Sure" columns, she recalled words from another song, one sent her by Maya Angelou. "When you have the chance to sit it out or dance, I hope you dance." With all that Oprah's "big life" offers her, it seems, at least for the foreseeable future, her choice will be to dance.

BIBLIOGRAPHY

BIOGRAPHICAL SOURCES

Adler, Bill. *The Uncommon Wisdom of Oprah Winfrey*. Secaucus, N.J.: Birch Lane Press, 1997.

Britt, Donna. "Patrice Takes Oprah to Church." *Washington Post*, 17 January 1995, B1.

Chapelle, Tony. "The Reigning Queen of TV Talk Oprah!" *Black Collegian* 21 (November–December 1990): 136. Quoted in Mr. Showbiz.

Clemetson, Lynette. "Oprah on Oprah." *Newsweek*, 8 January 2001, 38–48.

Dunn, Lois. L. "Oprah Winfrey." In *Notable Black Women*, edited by Jessie Carney Smith, 1273–76. Detroit: Gale Research, 1992.

"Giving a Hand to the Lefty of the Year." *Washington Post*, 30 November 1988, C2.

Harrison, Barbara Grizzuti. "The Importance of Being Oprah." *New York Times Magazine*, 11 June 1989, 28–36.

Hine, Darlene Clark, Elsa Barsley Brown, and Rosalyn Terborg-Penn, eds. *Black Women in America: An Historical Encyclopedia*, 2: 1274–76. Bloomington, Ind.: Carlson Publishing / Indiana University Press, 1993.

Jones, Quincy. *The Autobiography of Quincy Jones*. New York: Doubleday, 2001.

King, Norman. *Everybody Loves Oprah: Her Remarkable Life*. New York: Quill, William Morrow, 1987.

Lowe, Janet. *Oprah Speaks*. New York: John Wiley and Sons, 1998.

Mair, George. *Oprah Winfrey: The Real Story*. Secaucus, N.J.: Birch Lane Press, 1994.

Michaels, Bob, and Bob Hartlein. "Oprah: Who's My Real Father?" *Star*, 25 March 2003, 14–15.

Mr. Showbiz celebrity biographies. "Oprah Winfrey." http://mrshowbiz.go.com/celebrities/people/oprahwinfrey/bio.html (accessed 23 October 2001; site now discontinued).

Nelson, Jill. "The Man Who Saved Oprah." *Washington Post Magazine*, 14 December 1987, W 30.

Nelson, Jim, Alan Butterfield, and Reginald Fitz. "Oprah's Surprise Wedding." *National Enquirer*, 14 May 2002, 6–7.

"Oprah Winfrey: A Good Neighbor to Invite in for a Chat." *Newsday*, 10 September 1986, C1.

Roberts, Rozanne. "Honors." *Washington Post*, 3 December 2002, Cl, C4, C5.

Sellers, Patricia. "The Business of Being Oprah." *Fortune*, 1 April 2002, 50–64.

Tanner, Deborah. "Oprah Winfrey." *Time*, 8 June 1998, 196–98.

Taylor, B. Kimberly. "Oprah Winfrey." In *Contemporary Black Biography*, edited by Barbara Carlisle Bigelow, 2:262–65. Detroit: Gale Research, 1992.

Untitled photographs. *People*, 21 October 2002, 116–17.

Waldron, Robert. *Oprah!* New York: St. Martin's Press, 1987.

Winfrey, Oprah. Commencement Address, Wellesley College. Middletown, Conn. May 1998. http://wellesley.edu/publicaffairs/pahomepage/winfrey.html.

———. Interview by Larry King. CNN, 4 September 2001.

———. Interview by Mike Wallace. *60 Minutes*. CBS, 14 December 1986.

———. "Oprah Winfrey: Entertainment Executive." Interview on The Hall of Business' Web site. http://www.achievement.org. Chicago, Ill., 21 February 1991.

———. "The Power of One." Interview by Michael Logan. *TV Guide*, 4–10 October 2003, 37–40.

Zausner, Stephen. "Oprah's Got All That Money." *Facts on File*, 18 October 1993, 22.

Zoglin, Richard. "Lady with a Calling." *Time*, 8 August 1988, 62.

———. "People Sense the Realness." *Time*, 15 September 1986, 99.

BOOKS

Clark, Robert. Rev. of *A Hole in the Earth*, by Robert Bausch. *Washington Post*, 20 August 2000, X3.

Crandell, Ben. "Oprah's Shelved, So Others Must Pass on the Good Word." *South Florida's Sun Sentinel*, 12 April 2002, 76.

Elder, Robert K. "At 11, 'Heartsongs' Poet Turns Into a Publishing Phenom." *Orlando Sentinel*, 12 March 2003, E1, E3.

———. "Visit to 'Oprah Winfrey Show' Propels Book Status." *Orlando Sentinel*, 22 March 2003, E1, E3.

Franzen, Jonathan. *The Corrections*. New York: Farrar, Straus, and Giroux, 2001.
———. *How to Be Alone*. New York: Farrar, Straus, and Giroux, 2002.
———. Interview by Katie Couric. *Today Show*. NBC, New York, 19 November 2001.
———. "Meet Me in St. Louis." *New Yorker*, 4 December 2002, 70–75.
Giles, Jeff. "Errors and 'Corrections.' " *Newsweek*, 5 November 2001, 68–69.
Hitchens, Christopher. "Oprah, How About George?" *Palm Beach Post*, 1 March 2003, Dl.
Janz, Matt. "Out of the Gene Pool." *Washington Post*, 4 August 2002, SC 5.
Kirkpatrick, David. "Oprah Gaffe by Franzen Draws Ire and Sales." *New York Times*, 29 October 2001, E1, E3.
———. "Oprah Puts Book Club on Shelf." *Palm Beach Post*, 6 April 2002, 1A, 10A. (Rpt. from *New York Times*.)
Locayo, Richard. "Total Eclipse of the Heart." *Time*, 25 November 2002, 93.
Random House. "Thank You, Oprah." *New York Times*, 12 April 2002, B40.
Romano, Carlin. "For Oprah, Rough Work of Reviews Is Over." *Philadelphia Inquirer*, 9 April 2002, C1, C8.
Schwartz, Amy E. "Will Oprah Save the Book?" *Washington Post*, 15 December 1996, C7.
Simmons, Rachel. *Odd Girl Out: The Hidden Culture of Aggression in Girls*. New York: Harcourt, 2002.
Stamaty, Mark. "Boox." *New York Times Book Review*, 9 December 2001, 35.
Streitfeld, David. "Thousands Buy 'Reading Club' Books." *Washington Post*, 20 November 1996, D1.
Weeks, Linton. "Hallmark of a Poet." *Washington Post*, 11 May 2002, C1, C4.
———. "Oprah-Pick Franzen Wins National Book Award." *Washington Post*, 14 November 2001.
Yardley, Jonathan. "The Story of O." *Washington Post*, 29 October 2001, C2.
———. "The Story of O, Continued." *Washington Post*, 5 November 2001, C2.

OTHER MEDIA PERSONALITIES

Berenson, Alex. "Defining Martha Stewart's Alleged Crime." *New York Times*, 8 June 2003, Sec. 4: 5.
Carlson, Peter. "From Rosie O'Donnell." *Washington Post*, 5 June 2001, C2.
Knight, Jerry. "Not-So-Perfect-Performance Under Pressure." *Washington Post*, 9 June 2003, E1, E12.
"Martha Stewart's Woes Continue." *Palm Beach Post*, 1 May 2003, D7.
Masters, Brooke. "Stewart Prosecutor Balked at Insider-Trading Charges." *Washington Post*, 6 June 2003, E1.

Parks, Scott. "Not Quite a 'Lyman Mob.' " *Sun Sentinel,* 1 February 1998, 5H.

Singhania, Lisa. "Martha's Business Hurt by Insider Trading." *Palm Beach Post,* 5 March 2003, 1.

FILMS

Gilliam, Dorothy. "Black Men Ill-Served." *Washington Post,* 23 March 1989, C3.

———. "Breathing Easier with a Rare Film." *Washington Post,* 13 January 1996, B1.

Harrington, Richard. "Diluted 'Native Son.' " *Washington Post,* 16 January 1987, B8.

Kane, Gregory. "'Exhale' Adds to Bashing of Black Men." *Sun Sentinel,* 3 January 1996, B1.

Kempley, Rita. "Love's Labor Lost in 'Son.' " *Washington Post,* 16 January 1987, N17.

Shales, Tom. "'Morrie': Sugar with Zest of Lemon." *Washington Post,* 4 December 1999, C1.

FOOD, WEIGHT, AND EXERCISE

Carlson, Peter. "Meat from the Ground Up." *Washington Post,* 3 July 2001, C4.

"Catchy Viruses." *Washington Post,* 18 September 1995, F15.

Daley, Rosie. *In the Kitchen with Rosie.* New York: Alfred Knopf, 1996.

Greene, Bob. *Get with the Program.* New York: Simon and Schuster, 2002.

Hale-Shelton, Debra. "Oprah's Chef Puts Family Time on Menu." *Palm Beach Post,* 7 February 2002, FN1, FN3.

Lawson, Nigella. *How to Be a Domestic Goddess.* New York: Hyperion, 2001.

———. *How to Eat.* New York: John Wiley and Sons, 2000.

Lyman, Howard, with Glen Merzer. *Mad Cowboy.* New York: Scribner, 1998.

Mansfield, Stephanie. "Winfrey Taking on Donahue and a Diet, and Talking All the Way." *Washington Post,* 21 October 1986, D1.

Nelson, Jim, Reginald Fitz, and John Blossedr. "Oprah: I'm Out of Control." *National Enquirer,* 12 February 2002, 8–9.

Nelson, Jim, Alan Butterfield, and Reginald Fitz. "Oprah Soars to Deadly 275 Lbs." *National Enquirer,* 10 September 2002, 34–35.

Smith, Art. *Back to the Table: The Reunion of Food and Family.* New York: Hyperion, 2001.

"The Truth About Dieting." *Consumer Reports,* June 2002, 26–31.

FRIENDS

Als, Hilton. "Songbird." *New Yorker*, 5 August 2002, 72–76.

Angelou, Maya. *Even the Stars Look Lonesome*. New York: Random House, 1997.

———. *A Song Flung Up to Heaven*. New York: Random House, 2002.

———. *Wouldn't Take Nothing for My Journey Now*. New York: Random House, 1993.

Farhi, Paul. "With the President at the Gala, An Opera House United." *Washington Post*, 3 December 2002, C1, C4.

Graham, Stedman. *You Can Make It Happen*. New York: Simon and Schuster, 1997.

———. *You Can Make It Happen Every Day*. New York: Simon and Schuster, 1998.

Herz, Steve. "Oprah's Secret Plan to Disappear." *Globe*, 21 May 2002, 4–5.

Herz, Steve, Jeff Samuels, David Thompson, and Paul Lomax. "Oprah Gets the Boot from Stedman." *Globe*, 29 July 2003, 6, 7, 16.

Lupton, Mary. *Maya Angelou: Critical Companions to Popular Contemporary Writers*. Westport, Conn.: Greenwood Press, 1998.

Trescott, Jacqueline. "Quincy Jones: A Music Man Par Excellence." *Washington Post*, 2 December 2001, G1, G6, G7.

HOME

Koncius, Jura. "Stretching Out in Bed." *Washington Post*, 9 January 1997, T5.

Rogers, Patricia. "James Van Sweden at Home." *Washington Post*, 15 January 1998, T12.

———. "O's Meadow." *Washington Post*, "Home." 28 November 1991, 5.

HUMANITARIANISM AND KINDNESS

Barrientos, Tanya. "Oprah Winfrey to Get Anderson Award for Humanitarian Works." *Philadelphia Inquirer*, 11 February 2003, B1, B5.

Hanania, Ray. "Financial Profile: Oprah Winfrey: I'm Working for Charity Now." *Star Newspapers*, Apr. 1998: 1–7.

INFLUENCE

Gabler, Neal. *Winchell: Gossip, Power and the Culture of Celebrity*. New York: Alfred Knopf, 1995.

Moraes, Lisa de. "Could Clinton Be the Next Oprah? He's Been Talking to NBC." *Washington Post,* 3 May 2002, C1, C7.

LAWSUITS

Banesky, Sandy. "Deep in the Heart of Texas." *Sun Sentinel,* 29 January 1998, E1.
"Court Upholds Winfrey." *Washington Post,* 10 February 2000, A16.

MAGAZINES

Carlson, Peter. "Glossy and Greedy: Real Page-Turners." *Washington Post,* 3 December 2002, C1, C8.
———. "Women's Magazine Fades Out after 125 Year Identity Crisis." *Washington Post,* 20 February 2001, C1.
Winfrey, Oprah. "Oprah Talks to Quincy Jones." O, October 2001, 204, 207; 270–276.

TALK SHOWS

Anderson, Kurt. "Oprah and Jojo the Dog-Faced Boy." *Time,* 11 October 1993, 94.
Balz, Dan. "On 'Oprah' Relaxed Bush." *Washington Post,* 20 September 2001, A1.
Carlson, Peter. "The Heart of Talkness." *Washington Post Magazine,* 25 April 1993, 19–29.
Copeland, Libby. "In the Church of Feel-Good Pop Psychology." *Washington Post,* 26 June 2000, C1.
Dionne, E. J. "Chattering Class." *Washington Post,* 1 December 1996, W10.
Edwards, Ellen. "During Taping, TV Host Confesses." *Washington Post,* 13 January 1995, A1.
Ehrenreich, Barbara. "In Defense of Talk Shows." *Time,* 4 December 1995, 92.
Faludi, Susan. "The Money Shot." *New Yorker,* 30 October 1995, 64–87.
Grindstaff, Linda. *The Money Shot: Trash, Class, and the Making of TV Talk Shows.* Chicago: University of Chicago Press, 2002.
Kurtz, Howard. *Hot Air: All Talk, All the Time.* New York: Time Books, 1996.
Matusow, Barbara. "The Conversion of Bob Novak." *Washingtonian,* June 2003, 39–45.
McGraw, Phil. *Life Strategies.* New York: Hyperion, 1999.
Moraes, Lisa de. "Enriched Oxygen: Oprah Moving to Prime Time." *Washington Post,* 11 June 2002, C1.

Owers, Paul. "If Oprah Wears It, Watchers Will Buy." *Palm Beach Post*, 22 May 2003, 1D, 7D.

Peyser, Marc. "Paging Dr. Phil." *Newsweek*, 2 September 2002, 50–56.

Rice, Melinda. "Pharmacy Offers Dose of Old Skill." *Sun Sentinel*, 24 May 1998, B3.

Schemering, Christopher. "Queen of the Daytime." *Washington Post*, 18 September 1987, D12.

Scheuer, Jeffrey. *The Sound Bite Society*. New York: Routledge, 2002.

Shattuc, Jean. *The Talking Cure: TV Shows and Women*. New York: Routledge, 1997.

Whitbourne, Kathryn. "Elbowing In to Some Airtime on Oprah." *South Florida Sun-Sentinel*, 5 May 2003, 1D, 6D.

RACIAL MATTERS

Erstein, Hap. "Civil Rights Icon an Irresistible Subject." *Palm Beach Post*, 21 March 2003, 41.

Jefferson, Margo. "The Color Brown." Review of *Brown: The Last Discovery of America*, by Richard Rogriguez. *New York Times Book Review*, 16 February 2003, 27.

Mulgeta, Samson. "Crossing the Color Line." *Newsday*, 16 June 2002, A14.

Peck, Janice. "Talk About Race: Framing a Popular Discourse on 'Oprah Winfrey.' " *Cultural Critique* (Spring 1994): 89–126.

INDEX

About the Author

HELEN S. GARSON is the author of *Tom Clancy: A Critical Companion* (Greenwood 1996).